Food for
Good Health

Food for
Good Health

hamlyn

NOTES

All recipes have been analysed per serving by a professional nutritionist.

Both metric and imperial measurements have been given in all recipes. Use one set of measurements only and not a mixture of both.

Standard level spoon measurements are used in all recipes.
1 tablespoon = one 15 ml spoon
1 teaspoon = one 5 ml spoon

Eggs should be medium to large unless otherwise stated. The Department of Health advises that eggs should not be consumed raw. This book contains dishes made with raw or lightly cooked eggs. It is prudent for more vulnerable people such as pregnant and nursing mothers, invalids, the elderly, babies and young children to avoid uncooked or lightly cooked dishes made with eggs. Once prepared, these dishes should be kept refrigerated and used promptly.

Milk should be full fat unless otherwise stated.

Poultry should be cooked thoroughly. To test if poultry is cooked, pierce the flesh through the thickest part with a skewer or fork – the juices should run clear, never pink or red.

Do not re-freeze a dish that has been frozen previously.

Pepper should be freshly ground black pepper unless otherwise stated.

Fresh herbs should be used, unless otherwise stated. If unavailable, use dried herbs as an alternative, but halve the quantities stated.

Measurements for canned food have been given as a standard metric equivalent.

Nut and Nut Derivatives
This book includes dishes made with nuts and nut derivatives. It is advisable for customers with known allergic reactions to nuts and nut derivatives and those who may be potentially vulnerable to these allergies, such as pregnant and nursing mothers, invalids, the elderly, babies and children to avoid dishes made with nuts and nut oils. It is also prudent to check the labels of pre-prepared ingredients for the possible inclusion of nut derivatives.

Ovens should be pre-heated to the specified temperature — if using a fan-assisted oven, follow the manufacturer's instructions for adjusting the time and the temperature.

Contents

Introduction

A healthy diet is primarily about balance. Our bodies need certain amounts of minerals and vitamins in order to function properly and, by eating sensibly, this is easy to achieve. With busy lifestyles and stressful jobs, it is all too easy to neglect our diets. However, it is well worth taking the time to think about what you eat, as a sensible diet will boost energy and vitality and doesn't necessarily mean hours of preparation and cooking. Many of the recipes in this book can be prepared in advance or rustled up quickly at the end of a long day, whilst others can be saved for special occasions. Healthy eating does not mean compromising on enjoyable foods or cutting out treats, it simply means that you should be aware of the food you eat and follow a few simple guidelines.

Eight guidelines for a healthy diet

1. Enjoy your food

Food should be one of life's pleasures, to be savoured and enjoyed. There is enough stress in life already without adding to it by worrying unnecessarily about food. It is worthwhile to take time to enjoy food with family and friends and to be a bit adventurous in trying new recipes and new ways of cooking.

2. Eat a variety of different foods

There is no one food that will provide all the nutrients we need. (Apart from human milk which provides for a baby's needs in the first few months of life.) For this reason it is important to eat a wide variety of foods, and to make sure we include foods from all of the main food groups (see page 14).

3. Eat the right amount to be a healthy weight

Body weight is the result of the balance between the amount of energy (usually measured in Calories) taken in and the amount used up. People who eat more Calories than they use will gain weight.

The more physically active you are, the greater your energy need. It is sensible for all of us to increase our activity level, and thus our energy expenditure, to improve our health and well-being. By cutting down very strictly on food intake to keep body weight down, not enough of the essential nutrients will be eaten. A healthy balance of food and exercise is the best plan.

4. Eat plenty of foods rich in starch and fibre

Most people do not eat enough starchy foods, but these foods are valuable sources of fibre, especially wholegrain

manufacture these fatty acids, and they have to be eaten in our diets. Some fats are good sources of important vitamins, and fat helps to make our diets more palatable and interesting.

There is evidence that too high a proportion of fat in the diet leads to coronary heart disease – another reason to limit the amount of fat we eat.

There are several different kinds of fat and these may have different effects on the cholesterol level of our blood, but it is important to remember that the energy (Calorie) content of all fat is the same (see page 132).

The most important thing is to reduce the total amount of fat in the diet and then decide what kind of fat you want to use within that reduced amount.

cereals. These foods are also very versatile and can be used in lots of different, interesting ways (see pages 32 and 84).

To get a well-balanced diet you should have plenty of the starchy foods, at two, or preferably three, meals daily. When you have a main meal, most of the space on the plate should be taken up with starchy foods and vegetables, with the meat or alternative being quite a small amount in proportion.

5. Eat plenty of fruit and vegetables

Fruit and vegetables are protective foods, because they contain vitamins and minerals, which help to keep us healthy. They may also protect us from other diseases, such as coronary heart disease, and some forms of cancer. It is advised that we eat five portions of fruit and vegetables a day (see page 204) and with such a wide variety now available in the shops, and so many delicious recipes in this book that contain different types of fruit and vegetables, this should be no problem at all.

6. Cut down on foods containing a lot of fat

A certain amount of fat is essential in our diets and in particular we need small amounts of the so-called 'essential fatty acids'. This means that our bodies cannot

7. Don't have sugary foods and drinks too often

Most of us enjoy the taste of sweet things, but if sweet foods are eaten only at meal times it will help to protect our teeth.

Sugar (white, brown, honey, syrup) provides energy (Calories) but very little in the way of other nutrients. That is why it is sensible for people who are overweight to cut right down on their intake of sugar and sugary foods, in order to maintain health in the long term.

8. If you drink alcohol, drink sensibly

For most people alcohol is something to be enjoyed and it can enhance the pleasure at a meal or on a social occasion. Research has shown that a certain amount of alcohol may improve some aspects of our health. However, moderation is the important aspect to remember, as there are also a number of risks which are associated with drinking alcohol and it is sensible to know the limits and not to exceed these.

Vitamins

If you eat a wide variety of food and a balanced diet you should get all the vitamins you require, with no need for supplements. If you do take a supplement, it is sensible not to exceed the recommended dose. There are two main types of vitamins; fat-soluble and water-soluble. The fat-soluble vitamins, A, D and E, are stored in the body and taking excessive amounts could be harmful. The water-soluble vitamins, C and the B complex, are not stored in the body and any excess amounts are excreted in the urine. A good mixed diet should contain adequate amounts of all these vitamins.

Vitamin A (retinol)

Vitamin A is essential for vision in dim light and for the maintenance of healthy skin and surface tissues of the body. It is stored in the liver and is toxic in very excessive amounts. Vitamin A is found in natural fats, such as milk and butter, and liver has a very high content. It can also be made in the body from carotene, which is found in red and yellow vegetables such as carrots and peppers.

Vitamin D (cholecalciferol)

Vitamin D is essential for maintaining the right level of calcium and phosphorus in the blood and for building healthy bones and teeth. Deficiency causes rickets in children and osteomalacia (bone thinning) in adults.

The best source of Vitamin D is the action of sunlight on the skin. Dietary sources are less important, except for people who cannot go out or who do not expose their skin to light. Sources include fatty fish, milk, butter and egg yolks. Vitamin D is added to margarine, and some manufacturers add Vitamin D to breakfast cereals and some types of yogurt.

Vitamin C

Vitamin C is necessary for growth and the maintenance of healthy connective tissue in the body. Lack of Vitamin C leads to gum bleeding, bruising and poor wound healing. Only humans and guinea pigs need to get Vitamin C from their diet. All other animals can make the vitamin within their bodies.

The best sources of Vitamin C are vegetables and fruit. Potatoes are a good source of the vitamin because of the large amounts eaten. Blackcurrants are very high in the vitamin and citrus fruits are good sources. Green salads and vegetables are also useful.

The amount of Vitamin C in fruits and vegetables diminishes with storing and cooking. Frozen vegetables may therefore sometimes have a higher Vitamin C content than fresh vegetables which have been stored for some time.

Vitamin B

The Vitamin B complex includes thiamin (B1), riboflavin (B2) and niacin, also Vitamin B6 (pyridoxine), B12, biotin, pantothenic acid and folic acid.

Thiamin, riboflavin and niacin are essential for the release of energy from the food we eat, particularly from carbohydrate.

These vitamins are widely distributed in foods, including milk, offal, eggs, vegetables, fruit and wholegrain cereals. Many breakfast cereals are fortified with B Vitamins.

Vitamin B6 (pyridoxine) is involved in the metabolism of amino acids (the breakdown products of protein), and is necessary for the formation of haemoglobin. Deficiency of B6 is rare, and very high intakes could be dangerous. It occurs widely in food, especially in meat, fish, eggs, wholegrain cereals and some vegetables.

Vitamin B12 is a mixture of compounds, and is necessary (with folic acid) for the development and maintenance of cells in the blood. It occurs only in animal products, particularly liver, eggs, cheese, milk, meat and fish. It is also available from yeast extracts, and is added to some breakfast cereals. Deficiency leads to a form of anaemia.

Folic acid has a number of functions, but is important for the development of rapidly dividing cells. Folic acid deficiency can arise from poor diet, and also when there are increased needs for the synthesis of red blood cells, for example in pregnancy. There is some evidence that adequate folic acid in the diet can protect against the development of spina bifida in the very early stages of pregnancy. The best dietary sources of folic acid are offal and leafy green vegetables. Folic acid is easily destroyed by cooking vegetables, as it is lost in the water used.

Minerals

Calcium

Calcium is an important nutrient in our diets because adequate amounts are needed for the development of strong bones and teeth. Milk and milk products are the best sources of calcium in the diet. The calcium in milk is in the watery part of the liquids, so using skimmed or semi-skimmed milk, or low fat yogurts and cheeses will not lower your calcium intake.

For people who do not take milk, calcium is available in some vegetables and seeds. Some kinds of soya milk have added calcium. It is important for everyone to have a certain amount of calcium in the diet, particularly in childhood and early adulthood, when the bones are growing actively.

Iron

Iron is needed to keep the haemoglobin in blood to a healthy level. The best sources of iron in the diet are foods such as red meat and liver, but for vegetarians iron can be absorbed from beans and other pulses and from vegetables and cereals. Iron is absorbed better if you eat food containing Vitamin C at the same time (salad, tomatoes, fruit juice). Drinking tea with meals can inhibit the absorption of iron.

Nutritional information

Every recipe in this book has been nutritionally analysed with the amounts (per portion) displayed below each recipe. Symbols appear at the top of each page to highlight recipes that are good sources of iron, calcium or fibre; in addition, every recipe is low in fat, containing no more than 15 g of fat per portion, with some as low as 5 g. It is important to note that anything listed as 'optional' in the ingredients column has not been included in the nutritional analysis.

Symbols

The symbols used throughout this book relate to the following measurements:

Fat

♥	each portion contains 15 g or less
♥♥	each portion contains 12 g or less
♥♥♥	each portion contains 5 g or less

Fibre

▲	each portion contains 6 g or less
▲▲	each portion contains 12 g or less
▲▲▲	each portion contains 18 g or less

Iron

■	each portion contains at least 3 mg
■■	each portion contains at least 6 mg
■■■	each portion contains at least 9 mg

Calcium

●	each portion contains at least 100 mg
●●	each portion contains at least 200 mg
●●●	each portion contains at least 300 mg

These symbols and the measurements are designed to provide an easy referencing system when choosing recipes. This allows you to combine a number of different dishes throughout the day that have different nutritional benefits. For example, a breakfast that is high in fibre, or a main meal that contains a lot of iron.

"a sensible diet will boost energy and vitality and doesn't necessarily mean hours of preparation and cooking."

Fresh stock recipes

You will find it useful to refer to these basic recipes as they are required throughout the book. When making fish stock you should be able to find the bones you need at the fishmonger.

Once made, the stocks can be frozen when cooled. Freeze in small batches in plastic tubs or ice cube trays. When frozen, the cubes can be transferred to clearly labelled plastic bags for ease of storage.

Chicken stock

• Chop a cooked chicken carcass into 3 or 4 pieces and place it in a large saucepan with the raw giblets and trimmings, 1 roughly chopped onion, 2 large roughly chopped carrots and 1 roughly chopped celery stalk, 1 bay leaf, a few lightly crushed parsley stalks, 1 sprig of thyme and cover with 1.8 litres/3 pints cold water.
• Bring to the boil, removing any scum from the surface. Lower the heat and simmer for 2–2½ hours. Strain the stock through a muslin-lined sieve and leave to cool completely before refrigerating.

Makes 1 litre/1¾ pints
Preparation time: 5–10 minutes
Cooking time: about 2½ hours

Vegetable stock

• Place 500 g/1 lb chopped mixed vegetables, such as carrots, leeks, celery, onions and mushrooms in a saucepan, using about an equal quantity of each one, and add 1 garlic clove, 6 peppercorns, 1 bouquet garni (2 parsley sprigs, 2 thyme sprigs and 1 bay leaf). Cover with 1.2 litres/2 pints water. Bring to the boil and simmer gently for 30 minutes, skimming when necessary. Strain the stock and cool it completely before refrigerating.

Makes 1 litre/1¾ pints
Preparation time: 5–10 minutes
Cooking time: about 45 minutes

Fish stock

When purchasing the bones for this stock, avoid buying the bones of oily fish. It is very important that the stock does not boil as it will become very cloudy.
• Place 1½ kg/3 lb fish trimmings and 1 sliced onion, the white part of 1 small leek, 1 celery stalk, 1 bay leaf, 6 parsley stalks, 10 whole peppercorns and 475 ml/ 16 fl oz dry white wine in a large saucepan, and cover with 1.8 litres/3 pints cold water. Bring slowly to just below boiling point. Simmer for 20 minutes, removing any scum from the surface. Strain the stock through a muslin-lined sieve and leave to cool before refrigerating.

Makes 1.8 litres/3 pints
Preparation time: 10 minutes
Cooking time: 30 minutes

Daily Menus

It is important to eat a variety of food throughout the day, in order to obtain the required amounts of vitamins and minerals.

The following three daily menus have all been analysed, to give a percentage of the daily requirement of the listed nutrients provided by each meal. A total percentage is also shown, for all the meals in the day. These menus provide examples of the balance of foods that is required on a daily basis. The items that are highlighted in bold are recipes that can be found in this book.

Daily Menu 1

Breakfast orange juice
coffee with semi-skimmed milk
wheatgerm honey raisin muffin

Lunch **Greek Pita Wraps**
Tomatoes with Light French Dressing
Banana

Dinner **Hot Spiced Stew**
Vegetable Carpaccio
Fruit and Nut Crumble

Percentage of daily requirements provided by each meal:

	Protein	Energy (kilocalories)	Fibre	Calcium	Iron	Zinc	Vitamin C	Thiamin	Riboflavin	Niacin	Vitamin B6	Vitamin B12	Folate	Vitamin A
breakfast	14	10	9	15	10	27	123	40	23	16	63	31	31	12
lunch	50	31	30	35	26	39	120	62	30	42	97	55	45	43
dinner	76	50	111	52	96	82	289	142	44	62	311	9	124	59
total	140	91	150	102	132	148	532	244	97	120	471	95	200	114

Daily Menu 2

Brunch **Hot fruit salad** and yogurt
**Smoked Salmon and Poached Egg
  Salad Muffin**
Wholemeal bread and butter
Tea with semi-skimmed milk

Snack 1 apple

Dinner **Beetroot Borscht
Chicken with Ginger
Stir-fried Chinese Leaves**
Boiled white rice
Wholemeal Pear Tart

Daily Menu 3

Breakfast **3 tablespoons Granola**
Banana and Yogurt
Wholemeal bread with polyunsaturated
  margarine and marmalade
Tea with semi-skimmed milk

Lunch Apple Juice
Rocket, Tuna and Bean Salad
Crusty White bread

Dinner **Caldo Verde
Lentil Moussaka**
crusty white bread
Lychee and Apricot Compôte

Daily Menu 2

	Protein	Energy (kilocalories)	Fibre	Calcium	Iron	Zinc	Vitamin C	Thiamin	Riboflavin	Niacin	Vitamin B6	Vitamin B12	Folate	Vitamin A
brunch	92	42	55	67	48	54	47	72	84	80	75	121	56	60
snack	1	2	10	1	1	1	15	4	2	1	9	0	1	1
dinner	76	43	53	29	35	49	257	68	26	95	158	10	163	68
total	169	87	118	97	84	104	319	144	112	176	242	131	220	129

Daily Menu 3

	Protein	Energy (kilocalories)	Fibre	Calcium	Iron	Zinc	Vitamin C	Thiamin	Riboflavin	Niacin	Vitamin B6	Vitamin B12	Folate	Vitamin A
breakfast	38	30	33	51	25	46	29	66	44	23	72	23	35	17
lunch	64	28	20	42	43	32	133	59	25	87	83	143	52	59
dinner	76	38	94	51	88	69	390	112	63	48	234	87	122	56
total	178	96	147	144	156	147	552	237	132	158	389	253	209	132

The Food Pyramid

Healthy eating

This is all about eating a wide variety of foods, from each of the major food groups. The pyramid opposite is made up of these groups and shows the proportion that each of them should make up in our diet.

Food groups

The large base section of the pyramid contains the staple, starchy, carbohydrate foods, which should provide the major source of energy in the diet. These include cereals (such as wheat, rye, oats, barley), rice and products made from them. Other staple carbohydrate foods include potatoes, yams and other starchy vegetables. On the next step of the pyramid are fruit and vegetables. These provide many of the essential vitamins and minerals that we need. The third step of the pyramid contains the protein and dairy foods. Protein foods can come from animal or vegetable sources. Animal sources include meat, fish and eggs and also milk, cheese and yogurt. Good sources of vegetable protein foods are pulses, such as beans and lentils, and seeds.

Dairy products

Products such as milk, yogurt and cheese are good sources of protein and also provide essential minerals and vitamins. Milk is a very important source of calcium and also of the B Vitamin riboflavin. If you use low-fat dairy products you will lose much of the content of fat soluble Vitamins (A, D, E), but the essential minerals such as calcium will still be available.

Foods to avoid

Eat least of the foods in the top section of the pyramid, as these are high in fat or refined carbohydrate such as sugar and honey. These make food taste good and most of us enjoy the sensation of sweetness in food. However, sugars provide Calories (energy) and very little in the way of other nutrients. Too much sugar can result in weight gain and tooth decay.

Daily balance

Eat foods from each section of the pyramid every day, to get a balance of the necessary nutrients. For good nutrition we have to think of both quality and quantity. The amount we eat of certain foods, and how often we eat them, is very important for a healthy diet.

Quantities

For a balanced diet aim to have:

Starchy foods
4–5 servings daily
1 serving:
1 large slice of bread
1 medium bowl pasta or rice
1 bowl breakfast cereal
2 medium size potatoes or equivalent in yams, etc.

Fruit and vegetables
5 servings daily
1 serving could be:
1 apple, orange, banana or pear
1 dessert bowl of salad
1 portion fresh or frozen vegetables (about 75 g/3 oz)
1 small bowl of canned fruit in fruit juice
1 glass of fresh fruit juice

Protein and dairy foods
2–3 servings daily
One serving could be:
1 small portion of meat (50–75 g/2–3 oz)
1 portion of fish (125–150 g/4–5 oz)
1 egg
25 g/1 oz hard cheese
600 ml/1 pint milk or yogurt
cooked lentils or other pulses (175–200 g/6–7 oz)

Sugars and fats
1 serving daily
One serving could include a small amount of spreading or cooking fat, and/or a small amount of sugary food. Sugar is best included in a starchy item, such as a cake or biscuit, rather than on its own.

Sugars and fats

Protein and dairy foods

Fruit and vegetables

Starchy foods

Cook's Tools

Pasta spoon
This is a large stainless steel or plastic spoon which is ideal for serving all types of pasta. The teeth make it good for gripping long, thin pasta shapes such as spaghetti or tagliatelle and the hole in the centre allows the liquid to drain away.

Skimmer
A long-handled, shallow perforated spoon used for removing fat from stews and draining fried food. It helps reduce the amount of fat that is eaten. It can also be used for removing meat, chicken and fish from marinades or vegetables from boiling water..

Steamer
A saucepan with one or two perforated stacking steamers that fit snugly on top. The lower part of the saucepan can be used to cook pasta, rice or stews and the heat from this is used to steam vegetables above. Steaming food helps to keep vitamin loss to a minimum.

Mortar and pestle
A bowl and grinder used to crush spices to a fine powder or fresh herbs to a pulp for use in dressings, sauces and marinades. The mortar can be made of stone, wood or metal and comes in many sizes; its inside should be rough and unglazed.

Citrus juicer
Freshly-squeezed lemon, lime and orange juice is required in many recipes and is far superior to bought juices. The juicer makes it simple to extract the juice as it is needed and the rind of the fruit can be reserved and used later.

Measuring cups
These are used for measuring dry ingredients by their volume. They are quick and simple to use. However, this method is not as accurate as measuring ingredients by weight.

Wok
The wok is becoming an increasingly popular cooking utensil. Stir-frying involves cooking food rapidly over a high heat, using a small amount of oil and stirring all the time. It is a healthy way of cooking, as little oil is used and vegetables are cooked quickly, so they retain much of their vitamin content. Woks can also be used for braising and steaming.

Spatulas
Wooden spatulas are recommended for stir-frying as they do not damage the surface of the wok.

Knives
A good set of knives should last a lifetime if properly cared for. Knives come in all shapes and sizes and each one is designed for a different job. Essential ones are a small paring knife for peeling and trimming vegetables; a large, wide-bladed chopping knife for preparing a variety of foods; and a long serrated knife for slicing bread, cakes and pastry dishes. Wash and dry knives after use and keep them sharp to make them easier to use, and avoid unnecessary accidents.

Chopping board
These should be made from a material that is soft enough not to blunt a knife but hard enough not to splinter. They are generally made from wood or a synthetic material. Synthetic boards are easier to keep clean and sterile than wooden boards. Your chopping board should be as large as possible.

Griddle pan
This is a heavy cast-iron pan in which food can be cooked without using butter or oil. Griddling has become popular recently as it results in food that tastes good as well as being healthy.

Pasta spoon

Steamer

Skimmer

Mortar and pestle

Wooden spatulas

Citrus juicer

Wok

Measuring cups

Knives

FUSION
home

FUSION
home

Chopping board

Griddle pan

Breakfast

It has often been said that breakfast is the most important meal of the day.
It is certainly advisable to eat something before embarking on the day and
it also provides an opportunity to relax and get the day off to a good start.
In this chapter there are ideas for leisurely breakfasts, both hot and cold,
as well as recipes for quick breakfasts and some that can be prepared in
advance and picked up on the way out of the house.

Hot Fruit Salad

175 g/6 oz dried apricots
150 g/5 oz dried prunes
150 g/5 oz dried figs
600 ml/1 pint apple juice
2 tablespoons Calvados or brandy (optional)
low-fat natural yogurt, to serve (optional)
25 g/1 oz walnuts, coarsely chopped

place the dried fruits in a bowl with the apple juice and leave to soak overnight.

transfer to a saucepan and simmer for 10–15 minutes. Turn into a bowl and pour over the Calvados or brandy, if using. Serve immediately with low-fat natural yogurt, if liked, and sprinkled with the walnuts.

Serves 6
Preparation time: *10 minutes, plus soaking*
Cooking time: *10–15 minutes*

FACT FILE • Dried fruits are rich in potassium, which is an essential element in the diet. Potassium is involved in the function of body cells, and is needed for growth and repair of lean body tissue. All animal proteins are good sources of potassium. For vegetarians, good sources are potatoes, Brussels sprouts, cauliflower, peas and mushrooms.

carbohydrate 46 g • protein 4 g • kJ 968 • Kcal 228

Granola

100 ml/3½ fl oz safflower oil
40 ml/1½ fl oz malt extract
75 ml/3 fl oz clear honey
325 g/11 oz rolled oats
250 g/8 oz jumbo oats (large oat flakes)
50 g/2 oz hazelnuts
25 g/1 oz desiccated coconut
50 g/2 oz sunflower seeds
25 g/1 oz sesame seeds

place the oil, malt and honey in a large saucepan and heat gently until the malt is runny. Mix in the remaining ingredients and stir thoroughly.

turn into a large roasting pan and bake in a preheated oven at 190°C/375°F/Gas Mark 5 for about 20 minutes, stirring occasionally, until golden brown. Leave to cool, then separate into pieces with your fingers.

store in an airtight container. Serve with natural yogurt at breakfast time, or use as a topping for fresh fruit salad or stewed fruits.

Serves 18 (3 heaped tablespoons per portion)
Preparation time: *10 minutes, plus cooling*
Cooking time: *20 minutes*
Oven temperature: *190°C/375°F/Gas Mark 5*

FACT FILE • Malt extract is prepared from malted barley; it is a carbohydrate in which the main sugar is maltose. In some types of malt there is an enzyme present which was believed to aid the digestion of starchy foods, but today malt is used mainly to add flavour to breakfast cereals and other foods.

carbohydrate 30 g • protein 5 g • kJ 1023 • Kcal 243

Banana Muesli

125 g/4 oz rolled oats
50 g/2 oz sunflower seeds
300 ml/¹/₂ pint water
2 tablespoons clear honey
2 large bananas, peeled and sliced
250 g/8 oz black grapes, halved and deseeded
grated rind of 1 large orange
grated rind of 1 large lemon
50 g/2 oz flaked almonds, toasted

Garnish
pared strips of orange rind (optional)
pared strips of lemon rind (optional)

put the rolled oats and sunflower seeds into a bowl with the water and leave to soak overnight if possible.

mix well until creamy, then add the honey, bananas, grapes and orange and lemon rind. Spoon into a large serving dish or 4 small ones and sprinkle with toasted almonds. Serve garnished with orange and lemon rind, if liked.

Serves 4
Preparation time: *10 minutes, plus soaking*

FACT FILE • Many nuts are good sources of Vitamin E, and almonds have a particularly high content. Vitamin E is an anti-oxidant and there is some evidence that it may have a protective effect against coronary heart disease and some cancers.

carbohydrate 52 g • *protein 7 g* • *kJ 1373* • *Kcal 326*

Muesli Cake

175 g/6 oz muesli

125 g/4 oz molasses sugar

175 g/6 oz sultanas

2 tablespoons malt extract

250 ml/8 fl oz apple juice

2 cooking apples, peeled, cored and grated

175 g/6 oz wholemeal flour

3 teaspoons baking powder

11 walnut halves

1 tablespoon icing sugar (optional)

1 small bunch redcurrants, to serve

place the muesli, sugar, sultanas, malt extract and apple juice in a mixing bowl and leave to soak for 30 minutes. Add the apple and flour, sift in the baking powder and mix together thoroughly.

turn into a lined and greased 18 cm/7 inch round cake tin and arrange the walnuts around the edge. Bake in a preheated oven at 180°C/350°F/Gas Mark 4 for 1½–1¾ hours, or until a skewer inserted into the centre comes out clean. Leave the cake in the tin for a few minutes, then turn it out on to a wire rack to cool.

sift the icing sugar, if using, over the cooled cake and serve it with the redcurrants.

Serves 6
Preparation time: *15 minutes, plus soaking*
Cooking time: *1½–1¾ hours*
Oven temperature: *180°C/350°F/Gas Mark 4*

COOK'S FILE • A great cake for those who insist they don't have time to eat breakfast. If accompanied by orange juice, this makes a delicious and nutritious breakfast-on-the-go. Keep the cake in an airtight container or wrap the slices individually and store them in the freezer.

carbohydrate 88 g • protein 9 g • kJ 1926 • Kcal 454

Wheatgerm, Honey and Raisin Muffins

125 g/4 oz wheatgerm
2 teaspoons baking powder
pinch of salt
75 g/3 oz raisins
4 tablespoons clear honey
50 g/2 oz butter or margarine, melted
2 small eggs
about 6 tablespoons milk

put the wheatgerm, baking powder, salt and raisins into a bowl, then add the honey, butter or margarine, and eggs. Mix until blended, then stir in enough milk to make a fairly soft mixture which drops heavily from the spoon when you shake it.

put heaped tablespoons of the mixture into greased bun tins, dividing the mixture between the twelve sections. Bake in a preheated oven at 180°C/350°F/Gas Mark 4 for 15–20 minutes, until the muffins have puffed up and feel firm to a light touch. Serve warm.

Makes 12
Preparation time: *15 minutes*
Cooking time: *15–20 minutes*
Oven temperature: *180°C/350°F/Gas Mark 4*

FACT FILE • Wheatgerm comes from the embryo of the wheatgrain, where the essential nutrients for germination of the seed are stored. Wheatgerm is high in Vitamin E and the B Vitamins, all of which are needed for normal cell growth and metabolism.

carbohydrate 15 g • protein 4 g • kJ 493 • Kcal 117

Potato Cakes

500 g/1 lb potatoes, grated
1 onion, chopped
2 tablespoons chopped parsley
2 eggs, beaten
2 tablespoons olive oil
sea salt and pepper

put the grated potatoes into a colander and rinse under cold running water to remove excess starch.

place the potatoes in a bowl with the onion, parsley, eggs and salt and pepper to taste. Mix thoroughly.

heat the oil in a 20–23 cm/8–9 inch heavy-based frying pan. Add the potato mixture and pat lightly into a cake. Fry gently for about 8–10 minutes until the underside is crisp and brown.

slide the potato cake on to a plate then invert it back into the pan and fry the other side for 10 minutes until crisp and brown. Using a cutter, stamp the potato cake into rounds. Alternatively, cut the potato cake into wedges. Season with salt and pepper and serve immediately.

Serves 4
Preparation time: *10 minutes*
Cooking time: *about 16–20 minutes*

FACT FILE • Potatoes are a good source of Vitamin C in the diet, if eaten frequently and in medium to large portions. The amount is highest in new potatoes and falls gradually as they are stored. After three months storage the Vitamin C content of potatoes is less than half the original content.

carbohydrate 23 g • *protein 5 g* • *kJ 722* • *Kcal 172*

Good Sources of Fibre

Sources

We should all eat plenty of fibre in our diets, for fitness and well-being. The best sources of dietary fibre are the wholegrain cereal foods, such as wholemeal bread, wholegrain breakfast cereals, wholegrain pasta and brown rice. Vegetables, particularly pulses such as beans and lentils, are very good sources of fibre, and seeds and fruit also make an important contribution.

Dietary fibre

This is formed from the cell walls of plants and occurs in two forms, insoluble and soluble, which are both important for good health. In cereals the fibre is mainly insoluble, whereas in other cereals such as oats, barley and rye a higher proportion of the fibre is soluble. In fruit and vegetables the proportion of soluble to insoluble fibre is about equal. Dietary fibre is important in our diet to keep the bowel healthily active. A low-fibre diet causes constipation and over a period of time the bowel can lose its natural strength and elasticity. If there is little fibre in the diet, the transit time of food residue is slowed resulting in possible damage such as diverticulosis. This is the formation of small pockets in the lining of the gut. Too little fibre may also be a factor in the development of some forms of cancer. Fibre may also help to keep levels of blood fats down. It is recommended that we should eat about 18 g of dietary fibre every day.

Fibre content

Below is a list of some common foods and their fibre content.

Porridge, 1 medium bowl, *1 g*
Wholemeal bread, 1 slice, *2 g*
Eating apples, 1 medium, *2 g*
Cabbage, 1 medium serving, *2 g*
Branflakes, 1 small bowl, *4 g*
Baked beans, 1 medium
  serving, *5 g*

In this book, high fibre recipes are marked with a ▲ sign. One ▲ sign means a portion of food provides about 6 g fibre. Two ▲▲ signs mean a portion contains 12 g fibre, which is a high proportion of the daily dietary fibre requirement.

Wholegrain cereal

Wholemeal bread

Pear

Apple

Raspberries

Nuts

Prunes

Carrots

Parsnips

Dates

Lentils

Kidney beans

Beans

Mixed Rice Kedgeree *with Kippers*

75 g/3 oz wild rice

175 g/6 oz basmati rice

325 g/11 oz kipper fillets

25 g/1 oz butter

1 small onion, chopped

1 small garlic clove, chopped

grated rind and juice of 1 lemon

1 tablespoon hot curry paste

1 teaspoon ground turmeric

4 ripe tomatoes, skinned, deseeded and diced

50 g/2 oz sultanas

2 tablespoons chopped fresh coriander

2 tablespoons chopped parsley

salt and pepper

1 hard-boiled egg, shelled and quartered, to garnish

cook the wild rice according to packet instructions, and drain. Cook the basmati rice in plenty of lightly salted boiling water for 15 minutes; drain, refresh under cold water and drain again. Spread both rices on a baking sheet and leave to dry for 30 minutes.

steep the kippers in a bowl filled with boiling water for 8–10 minutes until they are cooked. Drain well and pat dry, skin the fillets and discard any large bones, then carefully flake the flesh.

melt the butter in a saucepan and fry the onion, garlic, lemon rind, curry paste and turmeric for 5 minutes, add the tomatoes and sultanas and fry for a further 10 minutes. Add the coriander and parsley, season with salt and pepper to taste and continue to stir over a low heat for 4–5 minutes until warmed through.

transfer the warmed rice to a large serving plate. Garnish with the egg quarters and serve immediately.

FACT FILE • Kippers are a fatty fish and a rich source of a particular type of polyunsaturated fat found only in the oils of such fish. These fish oils may protect against coronary heart disease. Kippers also contain Vitamins A and D.

Serves 4
Preparation time: 15 *minutes, plus drying*
Cooking time: *25–30 minutes*

carbohydrate 63 g • protein 29 g • kJ 2111 • Kcal 505

Smoked Salmon and Poached Egg Salad *on Blinis*

1 tablespoon distilled white vinegar
4 eggs
4 blinis (about 10 cm/4 inch diameter)
25 g/1 oz Anchovy Butter (see below)
200 g/7 oz smoked salmon
125 g/4 oz frisé lettuce
1 tablespoon poppy seeds
diced tomato, to serve (optional)
fresh chives, to garnish

Dressing

2 teaspoons Champagne or white wine vinegar
1 teaspoon Dijon mustard
1 tablespoon snipped chives
6 tablespoons extra virgin olive oil
2 ripe tomatoes, skinned, deseeded and diced
salt and pepper

COOK'S FILE • To make Anchovy Butter, purée 1–2 anchovy fillets using a mortar and pestle. Place in a bowl; add pepper, 2 teaspoons lemon juice and 25g /1oz unsalted butter. Mix with a fork.

bring a small frying pan of water to a gentle simmer, add the vinegar and then carefully break in the eggs to fit closely together. Remove the pan from the heat and leave the eggs in the water to poach until just set.

meanwhile, toast the blinis for 1 minute. Spread Anchovy Butter on one side.

blend together all the dressing ingredients except the tomatoes, season with salt and pepper to taste, and toss half of the dressing with the frisé lettuce. Stir the diced tomato into the remaining dressing.

arrange the blinis on serving plates, top each one with some smoked salmon and dressed frisé. Carefully remove the poached eggs from the water with a slotted spoon, drain on kitchen paper and sprinkle over the poppy seeds. Place 1 egg on top of each blini. Pour the tomato dressing around each blini and serve at once with diced tomato, if liked, and garnished with the chives.

Makes 4
Preparation time: *20 minutes*
Cooking time: *15 minutes*

carbohydrate 16 g • protein 23 g • kJ 1204 • Kcal 287

Lunches and Light Meals

What we eat for lunch is often dependent upon the other meals in the day; a more substantial or later breakfast might mean that a sandwich or fruit is adequate. On the other hand, lunch might be the main meal of the day, in which case, something a little more filling may be required. The recipes here cover all eventualities with sandwiches, salads, and pasta and rice dishes providing scope for a quick snack in the office or a more sociable occasion.

Greek Pitta Wraps

4 large pitta breads
125 g/4 oz cooked lamb, finely shredded
1 small bunch spring onions, trimmed and chopped
2 lettuce leaves, chopped
2 tomatoes, peeled, deseeded and chopped
4 black olives, halved and pitted
75 g/3 oz feta cheese, crumbled
4 lettuce leaves
salt and pepper

Dressing

2 tablespoons natural yogurt
2 tablespoons olive oil
¼ teaspoon Dijon mustard
¼ teaspoon honey
salt and pepper

carefully cut a slit across the top of each pitta bread. Gently open out each bread to form a pocket. Mix the dressing ingredients together in a small bowl, and season with salt and pepper to taste.

mix the lamb with the spring onions, chopped lettuce, tomatoes, olives, dressing and salt and pepper to taste, blending well.

divide the salad mixture and feta equally between the pitta pockets.

cook under a preheated moderate grill for about 2–3 minutes until the filling is bubbling, turning once. Add the fresh lettuce leaves and quickly roll up the pittas in greaseproof paper to serve.

Makes 4
Preparation time: *10 minutes*
Cooking time: *2–3 minutes*

FACT FILE • Feta cheese is made from sheep and goats' milk and has a higher water content than many hard cheeses. The fat and calorie content of feta is therefore quite a bit lower (by weight of portion) than that of, for example, Cheddar-type cheeses.

carbohydrate 58 g • *protein 20 g* • *kJ 1654* • *Kcal 390*

Prawns with Broccoli

250 g/8 oz cooked king prawns, peeled and deveined

1 slice fresh root ginger, peeled and thinly chopped

1 tablespoon medium or dry sherry

1 egg white

1 teaspoon cornflour

1½ tablespoons vegetable oil

2 spring onions, finely chopped

250 g/8 oz broccoli, divided into small florets and stems trimmed and sliced

1 teaspoon salt

1 teaspoon sugar

split each prawn in half lengthways and then cut into pieces.

put the prawns into a small bowl with the ginger, sherry, egg white and cornflour. Stir well and leave in the refrigerator to marinate for about 20 minutes.

heat 1 tablespoon of the oil in a large non-stick frying pan or wok and add the prawns. Stir-fry over a moderate heat for about 30 seconds. Remove from the pan with a slotted spoon and set aside.

heat the remaining oil in the frying pan. Add the spring onions and broccoli and stir well. Add the salt and sugar and stir-fry until the broccoli is just tender. Return the prawns to the wok and stir to mix with the broccoli. Serve immediately.

Serves 3
Preparation time: *10 minutes, plus marinating*
Cooking time: *5 minutes*

COOK'S FILE • The amount of time that food should be marinated for depends on the size of the item and the type of marinade. Cooked marinades should be allowed to cool first, whereas uncooked marinades can be used straight away.

carbohydrate 33 g • protein 11 g • kJ 1190 • Kcal 284

Grilled Pepperoni Baguette

I tablespoon olive oil
I small onion, chopped
I garlic clove, crushed
250 g/8 oz canned tomatoes, chopped
2 tablespoons tomato purée
I tablespoon oregano, finely chopped
2 small baguettes
50 g/2 oz pepperoni, thinly sliced
75 g/3 oz mozzerella cheese, sliced
4 black olives, halved and pitted
salt and pepper

heat the oil in a large frying pan and gently fry the onion and garlic for 5 minutes, until softened. Stir in the tomatoes, tomato purée, and oregano. Bring to the boil, reduce the heat and simmer until most of the liquid has evaporated.

slice the baguettes in half lengthways. Spread the tomato mixture evenly over the cut surface of the bottom halves of the baguettes, and season with salt and pepper to taste. Arrange the pepperoni slices, mozzarella, and olives on top.

place the baguette halves under a preheated moderate grill for 4–5 minutes, or until golden brown and bubbling. Cover with the tops of the baguettes and serve at once.

Serves 2
Preparation time: *20 minutes*
Cooking time: *14–15 minutes*

FACT FILE • Many people think wholemeal bread is much more nutritious than white bread, but this is not necessarily true. White bread is a good source of some minerals and vitamins, particularly if it is made from fortified flour to which calcium and iron have been added. Wholemeal bread contains less calcium and more B Vitamins.

carbohydrate 30 g • protein 10 g • kJ 1123g • Kcal 268g

Rocket, Tuna and Haricot Bean Salad

4 tomatoes, skinned, deseeded and roughly chopped

125 g/4 oz rocket

400 g/13 oz can haricot beans, drained

200 g/7 oz can tuna in spring water, drained

1 red onion, chopped

125 g/4 oz artichoke hearts in olive oil, drained except for 1 tablespoon of oil

2 young celery sticks with leaves, chopped

1 tablespoon pitted black olives

4 tablespoons lemon juice

1 tablespoon red wine vinegar

1/4 teaspoon crushed dried chillies

handful of flat leaf parsley, roughly chopped

salt and pepper

French bread, to serve (optional)

put the tomatoes into a large salad bowl with the rocket.

stir in the beans and tuna, roughly breaking the tuna into large chunks. Stir in the chopped red onion.

add the artichoke hearts, with 1 tablespoon of oil from the jar, the celery, olives, lemon juice, vinegar, chilli and parsley. Season with salt and pepper to taste.

mix all the ingredients together well and allow to stand for 30 minutes for the flavours to mingle. Serve the salad at room temperature with crusty bread, if liked.

Serves 4
Preparation time: *15 minutes, plus standing*

FACT FILE • Tuna may be bought canned in oil, brine or spring water. The advantage of the spring water variety is that it does not have added fat or salt. High salt intakes may be linked to high blood pressure and it is sensible to limit the amount of salt added to food.

carbohydrate 14 g • protein 17 g • kJ 668 • Kcal 158

Rustic Greek Salad

500–800 g/1 lb–1 lb 10 oz tomatoes (large, cherry or miniature plum)

200–250 g/7–8 oz feta cheese, drained and cut into 1 cm/½ inch cubes

1 small red onion (see method)

16 black Kalamata olives, pitted if preferred

25 flat leaf parsley leaves

2 tablespoons lemon juice

4 tablespoons light extra virgin olive oil

salt and pepper

if using large tomatoes, cut them in half lengthways, then cut each half into 3 wedges. If using cherry tomatoes, cut them in half lengthways. Put them into a large bowl with the feta.

cut the onion into quarters, then cut each quarter into 4 sections. Scatter over the tomatoes and cheese. Add the olives and parsley leaves.

pour over the lemon juice and toss very gently to coat. Use 2 wooden spoons or your fingers so as not to break the tomato flesh or the cheese. Pour over the oil, toss again and season with salt and pepper to taste. Serve the salad immediately.

Serves 8
Preparation time: *15 minutes*

FACT FILE • Olive oil is a good source of monounsaturated fats, which help to keep down the cholesterol level in the blood. For those who find olive oil too heavy, rapeseed oil is widely available. It is a light oil which is also high in monounsaturates.

carbohydrate 47 g • protein 12 g • kJ 1483 • Kcal 352

Pumpkin Soup
with Crusty Cheese Topping

1 tablespoon sunflower or olive oil

1 large onion, finely chopped

3 garlic cloves, crushed

2 celery sticks, chopped

750 g/1½ lb pumpkin flesh, roughly chopped

750 ml/1¼ pints Vegetable Stock (see page 11) or
Chicken Stock (see page 10)

pinch of grated nutmeg

1 bay leaf

a few parsley stalks

65 ml/2½ fl oz single cream

1–2 tablespoons finely chopped parsley, extra to
garnish

salt and pepper

single cream or crème fraîche, to serve (optional)

Garnish

1 small French stick

50 g/2 oz Gruyère or fontina cheese, grated

heat the oil in a saucepan and fry the onion and garlic until soft but not brown. Add the celery and pumpkin flesh and fry for 10–15 minutes to draw out the flavours. Stir in the stock and nutmeg. Tie the bay leaf and parsley stalks together with string, add to the saucepan and bring to the boil. Reduce the heat and simmer for about 30 minutes until the vegetables are soft.

remove the bouquet of herbs and purée the soup in a blender or food processor. Alternatively, pass it through a fine sieve. Return the purée to the saucepan, bring to the boil and season with salt and pepper. Stir in the cream and parsley, return to the boil, then reduce the heat and keep the soup warm while preparing the garnish.

cut the French bread into 8 slices, place on a baking sheet and toast under a preheated moderate grill until pale golden on both sides. Leave the grill on.

pour the hot soup into 4 deep ovenproof bowls. Arrange 2 pieces of French bread in each one, overlapping them slightly. Sprinkle the bread with grated cheese. Set the bowls on the baking sheet and cook quickly under the grill until the cheese is golden brown and bubbling. Garnish with parsley and a small swirl of single cream or crème fraîche, if liked. Serve immediately.

FACT FILE • Like many yellow or red vegetables pumpkin is a good source of carotene, from which our bodies can make Vitamin A. Vitamin A is important for the health of soft tissues and helps prevent night blindness.

Serves 4
Preparation time: *25 minutes*
Cooking time: *1¼ hours*

carbohydrate 46 g • protein 13 g • kJ 1417 • Kcal 337

Spinach and Chickpea Flan

300 g/10 oz ready-made shortcrust pastry
(or see Cook's File, below)
175 g/6 oz spinach leaves
1 tablespoon extra virgin olive oil
1 small onion, thinly sliced
2 garlic cloves, crushed
1 teaspoon ground turmeric
200 g/7 oz canned chickpeas, drained
2 eggs, lightly beaten
200 ml/7 fl oz semi-skimmed milk
pinch of grated nutmeg
salt and pepper

roll out the pastry on a lightly floured surface and use to line a deep, 20 cm/8 inch flan tin. Prick the base and chill for 20 minutes. Line with foil and fill with baking beans then bake in a preheated oven at 200°C/400°F/Gas Mark 6 for 10 minutes. Remove the foil and beans and bake for a further 10–12 minutes until the pastry is crisp.

meanwhile wash the spinach and place in a large saucepan. Heat gently for 3–4 minutes until the spinach wilts. Drain, squeeze out the excess liquid and chop finely.

heat the oil in a saucepan, add the onion, garlic and turmeric and fry for 5 minutes. Stir in the chickpeas and spinach then remove from the heat. Spread over the pastry case.

beat together the eggs, milk, nutmeg and salt and pepper and pour into the pastry case. Bake for 35–40 minutes until firm and golden.

COOK'S FILE • If you would like to make your own shortcrust pastry, sift 175 g /6 oz plain flour into a bowl with ½ teaspoon of salt. Rub in 75 g/3 oz diced butter until the mixture resembles fine breadcrumbs. Gradually work in enough cold water (between 2 and 3 tablespoons) to form a soft dough. Knead until smooth on a lightly floured surface.

Serves 8
Preparation time: *25 minutes, plus chilling*
Cooking time: *about 1 hour*
Oven temperature: *200°C/400°F/Gas Mark 6*

carbohydrate 24 g • *protein 7 g* • *kJ 1036* • *Kcal 248*

Farfalle

with Olives and Capers

300 g/10 oz farfalle

125 g/4 oz pitted black or green olives

2 pinches of crushed dried chillies

2 tablespoons capers, chopped

7 anchovy fillets, drained and chopped

4 large sun-dried tomato pieces in olive oil

large handful of parsley, chopped

50 g/2 oz Parmesan cheese, grated

salt and pepper

1 red chilli, deseeded and thinly sliced, to garnish

cook the farfalle in lightly salted boiling water, according to packet instructions.

roughly chop the olives and put them in a saucepan with the chillies, capers and anchovies. Chop the sun-dried tomatoes and add them to the pan with 1 tablespoon of oil from the jar. Gently heat the mixture for 4 minutes until warm; do not let it fry.

drain the pasta when cooked and transfer to a serving dish. Add the warm olive mixture to the pasta with the parsley and Parmesan. Season with salt and pepper to taste, then mix well and serve, garnished with the fresh chilli. This dish can also be left to stand for a while and served at room temperature.

Serves 4

Preparation time: *10 minutes*

Cooking time: *15 minutes*

COOK'S FILE • Although you can use almost any type of pasta to make a tasty dish, some sauce and pasta combinations work better than others. For instance, cream sauces cling well to small, ridged and hollow pasta shapes. Long pasta such as spaghetti and vermicelli are good choices for relatively dry butter, oil and tomato-based sauces. Pappardelle, tagliatelle and flat ribbon-shaped pastas work well with rich sauces.

carbohydrate 58 g • protein 16 g • kJ 1660 • Kcal 393

FAT ♥♥   FIBRE ▲   IRON ■   CALCIUM ●●

Rigatoni
with Tomato and Chilli

300 g/10 oz rigatoni
2 tablespoons olive oil
1 onion, chopped
2 garlic cloves, chopped
2 pinches of crushed dried chillies
10 plum tomatoes, skinned, deseeded and chopped
1 teaspoon sugar
1 teaspoon vinegar
handful of flat leaf parsley, chopped
salt and pepper
50 g/2 oz Parmesan cheese shavings, to serve

cook the rigatoni in lightly salted boiling water, according to packet instructions.

heat the oil in a saucepan and sauté the onion and garlic until soft but not brown. Add the chillies.

add the tomatoes to the onion mixture with the sugar and vinegar and season with salt and pepper to taste. Mix gently and simmer slowly for a few minutes.

drain the pasta when cooked. Stir the parsley into the tomato sauce, then add the sauce to the pasta and mix well. Serve immediately with the Parmesan shavings.

Serves 4
Preparation time: *10 minutes*
Cooking time: *15 minutes*

FACT FILE • One small tomato provides about one quarter of the daily requirement of Vitamin C. The Vitamin C content of fruits and vegetables diminishes with storage, preparation and cooking. Cook fresh tomatoes quickly and serve them immediately whenever possible. Some Vitamin C does remain in canned tomatoes and tomato purée.

carbohydrate 66 g • protein 16 g • kJ 1766 • Kcal 418

Green Herb Risotto

1 litre/1¾ pints Chicken Stock (see page 10) or
Vegetable Stock (see page 11)
25 g/1 oz butter
1 tablespoon olive oil
1 onion, finely chopped
1 garlic clove, chopped
300 g/10 oz arborio rice
handful of parsley, chopped
handful of basil, chopped
handful of oregano, chopped
handful of thyme, chopped
50 g/2 oz Parmesan cheese, grated
salt and pepper
sage sprigs, to garnish

heat the stock in a saucepan until it reaches a gentle simmer.

melt the butter with the olive oil in another saucepan, add the onion and garlic and sauté for 3 minutes.

add the rice, stir well to coat the grains with the butter and oil, then add a ladleful of hot stock, enough to cover the rice, and stir well. Simmer gently and stir the rice constantly, adding more stock as it is absorbed. Continue adding the stock and stirring until it has all been absorbed and the rice is cooked and coated in a creamy sauce.

add the chopped herbs and the Parmesan. Season with salt and pepper and stir well. Serve immediately, garnished with the sage sprigs.

Serves 4
Preparation time: *5 minutes*
Cooking time: *25–30 minutes*

FACT FILE • A proper risotto cannot be made without the correct rice. Many supermarkets sell Italian risotto rice and some sell the specific varieties, arborio or carnaroli. They all have the same vital characteristic in that the individual grains of rice can absorb a large quantity of liquid without losing their texture and becoming mushy.

carbohydrate 63 g • *protein 11 g* • *kJ 1716* • *Kcal 412*

Smoked Haddock Risotto

500 g/1 lb skinless smoked haddock fillet
1.2 litres/2 pints water
2–3 saffron threads
25 g/1 oz butter
4 shallots, finely chopped
2 garlic cloves, crushed
1 tablespoon chopped sage
375 g/12 oz arborio rice
150 ml/¼ pint dry white wine
4 tablespoons half-fat crème fraîche
25 g/1 oz Parmesan cheese, grated
salt and pepper
12 large basil or sage leaves, to garnish

pull out and discard any bones in the haddock. Place the fish in a large frying pan and pour in the water. Bring slowly to the boil and simmer gently for 5 minutes. Lift out the fish, flake into large pieces and set aside. Strain the liquid into a saucepan and add the saffron threads. Leave to infuse for 10 minutes.

melt the butter in a large, non-stick frying pan and fry the shallots, garlic and chopped sage for 5 minutes until softened but not brown. Add the rice and stir-fry for 1 minute until all the grains are glossy. Pour in the wine and boil rapidly for 5 minutes.

meanwhile, bring the saffron stock to a gentle simmer. Add a ladleful of stock to the rice, stir well and reduce the heat to a simmer. Stir the rice constantly, adding more stock as it is absorbed. Continue adding the stock and stirring until it has all been absorbed and the rice is cooked, but still retains a slight crunch in the centre. This will take about 20–25 minutes.

stir in the crème fraîche, cheese and salt and pepper and arrange the flaked fish on top. Serve the risotto garnished with the basil or sage leaves.

Serves 6
Preparation time: *10 minutes*
Cooking time: *35 minutes*

FOOD FACT • Smoked fish has a high salt content so it should be used only in limited quantities. Salt (sodium chloride) is essential for normal health, but most of us eat far more than we need. Over-indulgence in salt has been linked with high blood pressure, particularly in people who are also overweight.

carbohydrate 52 g • *protein 27 g* • *kJ 1860* • *Kcal 445*

Soups and Starters

A freshly prepared soup or a delicious starter is the perfect introduction to any meal, whether for a special family occasion or when entertaining friends. Many of the recipes here can be meals in their own right or served as a selection of snacks at an informal buffet.

Beetroot Borscht

with Soured Cream and Chives

750 g/1½ lb fresh raw beetroot, washed
1 carrot, grated
1 onion, grated
2 garlic cloves, crushed
1.5 litres/2½ pints Vegetable Stock (see page 11)
4 tablespoons lemon juice
2 tablespoons sugar
1 large cooked beetroot
salt and pepper

Garnish
150 ml/¼ pint soured cream
1 teaspoon snipped chives
whole chives

scrape young beetroot, or peel older ones with a potato peeler, then grate the flesh using a coarse grater into a large saucepan. Add the carrot, onion, garlic, stock, lemon juice and sugar and season with salt and pepper to taste. Bring to the boil. Cover the pan, reduce the heat and simmer for 45 minutes.

meanwhile, cut the whole cooked beetroot into matchsticks about 4 cm/1½ inches long. Cover and refrigerate until required.

when the soup vegetables are tender, strain the contents of the saucepan through a sieve lined with muslin. Discard the vegetables. (At this stage, the beetroot juice can be cooled and stored in the refrigerator until required. It will keep for several days. It can also be frozen.)

put the beetroot juice into a clean saucepan with the beetroot matchsticks. Gently bring to the boil, then simmer for a few minutes to warm the beetroot through. Season with salt and pepper to taste, ladle into warmed soup bowls and serve with a spoonful of soured cream on top and garnished with snipped chives and some whole chives tied in a small bundle.

FACT FILE • Although it is a red vegetable, beetroot is not a good source of carotene. It does have a high content of folic acid, although some of this will be lost in cooking. Pickled beetroot is low in folic acid because the vitamin drains into the pickling liquid, which is discarded.

Serves 6
Preparation time: *25 minutes*
Cooking time: *1 hour*

carbohydrate 20 g • protein 4 g • kJ 579 • Kcal 138

Gazpacho Andaluz

125 g/4 oz onion, finely diced

125 g/4 oz green pepper, cored, deseeded and finely diced

125 g/4 oz red pepper, cored, deseeded and finely diced

375 g/12 oz cucumber, peeled and finely diced

750 g/1½ lb well-flavoured red tomatoes, peeled, deseeded and coarsely chopped

400 g/13 oz can chopped plum tomatoes

3 garlic cloves, crushed

3 tablespoons double concentrate tomato purée

500 ml/17 fl oz tomato juice

150–300 ml/¼–½ pint water

1½ teaspoons soft brown sugar

1 teaspoon finely chopped oregano

5 tablespoons red wine vinegar

salt and pepper

chives, to garnish

Croûtons

3 slices bread

1½ tablespoons lemon juice

reserve about 4 tablespoons each of the onion, green and red peppers and cucumber for the garnish. Put the remaining diced vegetables into a food processor or blender with the fresh and canned tomatoes, garlic and tomato purée and blend until smooth.

add the tomato juice, water to taste, sugar, oregano and wine vinegar, then process again until well mixed. Season with salt and pepper. Transfer to a large bowl or measuring jug, cover and chill for at least 2 hours.

meanwhile, make the croûtons. Remove the crusts from 3 slices of bread. Brush both sides of the bread with lemon juice. Toast the bread until pale brown on both sides. Cut into cubes.

just before serving, divide the reserved diced vegetables between 8 chilled soup plates. Pour the cold soup on top. Serve with croûtons and garnished with chives.

Serves 8
Preparation time: *20 minutes, plus chilling*

FACT FILE • Colour makes a difference to the carotene content of peppers. Red peppers have a very high carotene content, whereas it is much lower in green and yellow peppers.

carbohydrate 11 g • *protein 3 g* • *kJ 245* • *Kcal 57*

Celery and Lovage Soup

with Herb Cream and Croûtons

25 g/1 oz butter
375 g/12 oz celery, chopped
1 large onion, roughly chopped
1 small leek, white part only, sliced
125 g/4 oz potatoes, cubed
14 large lovage leaves, chopped
750 ml/1¼ pints Vegetable Stock (see page 11) or
Chicken Stock (see page 10)
300 ml/½ pint skimmed milk
salt and pepper

Garnish

75 ml/3 fl oz whipping cream, lightly whipped
1 tablespoon finely chopped lovage,
1 tablespoon finely chopped parsley
1 tablespoon finely chopped chives
¼ teaspoon celery seeds
celery leaves
75 g/3 oz croûtons (see page 66)

melt the butter in a large, heavy-based saucepan. Add the celery, onion, leek and potatoes, cover closely with greaseproof paper and sweat over a gentle heat for 10–15 minutes until soft but not brown.

stir in the lovage leaves and pour in the stock and milk. Season with salt and pepper to taste and bring to the boil, then cover the pan and reduce the heat to a simmer. Cook for 20–25 minutes.

purée the soup in batches in a food processor or blender until smooth. Alternatively, pass it through a fine sieve. Return the soup to the pan, adjust the seasoning as necessary, and bring to the boil.

mix the cream with the chopped herbs, reserving a few. Pour the hot soup into warmed soup bowls, spoon a little herb cream on top of each one and sprinkle with the reserved herbs, celery seeds, leaves and croûtons.

Serves 6
Preparation time: *15 minutes*
Cooking time: *40–50 minutes*

COOK'S FILE • Lovage leaves have a similar taste to celery. The seeds of the plant can also be used as a flavouring.

carbohydrate 11 g • protein 4 g • kJ 570 • Kcal 137

Minted Green Pea Soup

with Paprika and Croûtons

1 tablespoon olive or sunflower oil

1 onion, chopped

2 celery sticks, chopped

1–2 teaspoons hot paprika

900 ml/1½ pints Vegetable Stock (see page 11) or Chicken Stock (see page 10)

750 g/1½ lb fresh or frozen peas

3 mint sprigs

1 tablespoon lime juice

150 ml/¼ pint half-fat crème fraîche

salt and pepper

Garnish

a little hot paprika

6 small mint sprigs

75 g/3 oz croûtons (see page 66)

heat the oil in a large saucepan and fry the onion and celery until soft but not brown. Stir in the paprika and fry for a few minutes. Bring the stock to the boil in another saucepan and add to the saucepan with the peas, mint and lime juice. Bring to the boil, then reduce the heat and simmer for 15–20 minutes until the peas are tender. If using frozen peas, cook for only 5–8 minutes. Do not overcook the peas or the soup will lose its bright green colour.

when the peas are soft, blend the soup in a food processor or blender until smooth. Alternatively, pass the soup through a fine sieve. Return the purée to the saucepan, bring to the boil and season with salt and pepper to taste. Remove from the heat and stir in two-thirds of the crème fraîche, then add a little extra stock, if necessary, to give the desired consistency. Warm through gently.

serve the soup in shallow soup bowls with the croûtons. Put a spoonful of crème fraîche in the centre of each bowl. Sprinkle a little paprika on top and garnish with a sprig of mint.

FACT FILE • Paprika is a seasoning ground from a sweet red pepper variety, that is said to be the plant which has the highest Vitamin C content.

Serves 6
Preparation time: *20 minutes*
Cooking time: *30–45 minutes*

carbohydrate 15 g • protein 9 g • kJ 660 • Kcal 158

Creamed Celeriac and Parmesan Soup

25 g/1 oz polyunsaturated margarine

2 large onions, roughly chopped

1 garlic clove, crushed

500 g/1 lb celeriac, peeled and roughly chopped

1.35 litres/2¼ pints Vegetable Stock (see page 11) or Chicken Stock (see page 10)

45 ml/1½ fl oz whipping cream

50 g/2 oz Parmesan cheese, grated, reserving a little to garnish

salt and pepper

flat leaf parsley sprigs, to garnish

melt the margarine in a large saucepan and fry the onion, garlic and celeriac over a gentle heat for 4–5 minutes to draw out the flavours without browning. Add the stock and bring to the boil. Reduce the heat to a simmer, cover and cook for 25–30 minutes until the celeriac is tender.

allow the soup to cool slightly, then blend in a food processor or blender, in batches, until smooth. Alternatively, pass through a fine sieve. Return the purée to the saucepan and add the cream and Parmesan. Reheat and simmer gently for a few minutes, stirring to blend. Season with salt and pepper to taste.

to serve, put a little of the remaining Parmesan in the bottom of each warmed soup bowl and pour on the hot soup. Serve garnished with black pepper, flat leaf parsley sprigs and the remaining grated Parmesan.

Serves 6
Preparation time: *15 minutes*
Cooking time: *35–40 minutes*

FACT FILE • Celeriac is a member of the celery family and has a large, fleshy root. It is easily digested and has a high phosphorus content.

carbohydrate 9 g • *protein 6 g* • *kJ 680* • *Kcal 165*

Roasted Pepper Soup *with Tomatoes, Garlic and Fragrant Herbs*

2 tablespoons olive oil

5 large red peppers, cored, deseeded and roughly chopped

1 kg/2 lb tomatoes, halved

2 large onions, roughly chopped

2 carrots, roughly chopped

2 celery sticks, chopped

10 large garlic cloves, peeled

2 small red chillies, deseeded and finely chopped

2 tablespoons double concentrate tomato purée

2 teaspoons finely chopped thyme

3 tablespoons finely shredded basil

2 tablespoons finely chopped flat leaf parsley

1.2–1.5 litres/2–2½ pints hot Vegetable Stock (see page 11)

1½ teaspoons brown sugar

Tabasco sauce (optional)

salt and pepper

Garnish

125 ml/4 fl oz low-fat crème fraîche

basil or flat leaf parsley sprigs

put the oil into a large roasting tin and heat on the top of the stove. Add the peppers, tomatoes, onions, carrots, celery, garlic and chillies and mix thoroughly. When the vegetables are sizzling hot, transfer them to a preheated oven at 200°C/400°F/Gas Mark 6 and cook for 1 hour, stirring occasionally. Remove the roasting tin from the oven, stir in the tomato purée and leave the vegetables to cool.

transfer the vegetables to a food processor or blender and blend in batches until very smooth. Push through a plastic sieve into a clean saucepan to remove any remaining skin and seeds.

put the thyme, basil and parsley into the food processor or blender with about 150 ml/¼ pint of the vegetable purée and blend until smooth. Add to the rest of the vegetable purée in the saucepan. Dilute with the vegetable stock to the desired consistency. Season with sugar, salt and pepper and a little Tabasco sauce, if liked. Serve in warmed soup bowls, garnished with a spoonful of crème fraîche and a sprig of basil or parsley.

Serves 8
Preparation time: *30 minutes*
Cooking time: *about 1¼ hours*
Oven temperature: *200°C/400°F/Gas Mark 6*

carbohydrate 21 g • protein 5 g • kJ 753 • Kcal 180

Thai Seafood Soup

4 kaffir lime leaves, or ¼ teaspoon grated lime rind
750 ml/1¼ pints Chicken Stock (see page 10) or Fish Stock (see page 11)
1 tablespoon Thai red curry paste
1 teaspoon salt
2 tablespoons Thai fish sauce (nam pla)
4 lemon grass stalks, finely chopped
5 galangal or ginger slices, finely chopped
125 g/4 oz cod fillet
125 g/4 oz raw prawns, shelled and deveined (see page 88)
125 g/4 oz crab claws
125 g/4 oz prepared squid, cut into bite-sized pieces
125 g/4 oz cooked mussels, shelled and debearded
4 Thai chillies, crushed
2 tablespoons lemon juice

Garnish
mint sprigs
1 tablespoon fresh coriander, chopped

remove the central ribs from the lime leaves, if using, dividing the leaves in half. Set aside.

mix 2 tablespoons of the stock with the curry paste in a small saucepan. Heat the mixture, stirring, until it forms a sauce. Keep the sauce warm until required.

bring the remaining stock to the boil in a large saucepan. Stir in the salt, fish sauce, lemon grass, lime leaves or grated lime rind and galangal or ginger.

add the fish and seafood to the stock, return the stock to the boil, then lower the heat and simmer gently for 5 minutes. Stir in the curry sauce, chillies and lemon juice, then transfer the soup to a serving bowl. Garnish with mint sprigs and chopped coriander and serve immediately.

Serves 4
Preparation time: *20 minutes*
Cooking time: *10 minutes*

FACT FILE • Seafood is a good source of iodine. A small amount of iodine is necessary in the diet for the prevention of goitre. Most people will get sufficient iodine from a varied diet which includes milk and seafood.

carbohydrate 3 g • protein 19 g • kJ 474 • Kcal 113

Caldo Verde

2 tablespoons olive oil

1 large onion, chopped

2 garlic cloves, chopped

500 g/1 lb potatoes, cut into 2.5 cm/1 inch cubes

1.2 litres/2 pints water or Vegetable Stock (see page 11)

250 g/8 oz spring greens, finely shredded

2 tablespoons chopped parsley

salt and pepper

croûtons (see page 66), to serve

heat the oil in a large frying pan and fry the onion for 5 minutes until softened but not brown. Add the garlic and potatoes and cook for a few minutes, stirring occasionally.

add the water or stock, season with salt and pepper to taste and cook for 15 minutes until the potatoes are tender. Mash the potatoes roughly in their liquid, then add the greens and boil uncovered for 10 minutes. Add the parsley and simmer for 2–3 minutes until heated through. Serve with long croûtons.

Serves 6

Preparation time: *10 minutes*

Cooking time: *40 minutes*

FACT FILE ● Like many green vegetables, spring greens contain folic acid, or folate. Folate is necessary for normal cell growth and for the prevention of a particular form of anaemia. The folate content of foods diminishes with storage, so choose leafy vegetables which are as fresh as possible.

carbohydrate 19 g ● *protein 4 g* ● *kJ 522* ● *Kcal 125*

Greek Vine Leaves
with Savoury Stuffing

425 g/14 oz can vine leaves
2 tablespoons olive oil
150 g/5 oz lean minced beef
1 large onion, finely chopped
¼ fennel bulb, grated
2 garlic cloves, crushed
150 g/5 oz cooked long-grain rice
1 tablespoon chopped dill
1 teaspoon dried oregano
150 ml/¼ pint dry red wine
150 ml/¼ pint water
4 tablespoons lemon juice
salt and pepper
lemon wedges, to serve

put the vine leaves in a sieve, rinse and drain thoroughly.

heat 1 tablespoon of the oil in a large frying pan. Add the minced meat, onion, fennel and garlic and fry, stirring, until cooked. This will take about 8–10 minutes. Stir in the rice, dill and oregano and season with salt and pepper to taste.

spread the mixture evenly over the vine leaves. Fold the long sides of the vine leaves over to secure the mixture and roll up securely from the shorter edge to make neat parcels.

mix the remaining oil, the red wine, water and lemon juice in a saucepan, add the stuffed vine leaves, cover, and cook over a gentle heat for about 20 minutes. Remove with a slotted spoon and serve with lemon wedges.

Serves 4
Preparation time: *15 minutes*
Cooking time: *30 minutes*

COOK'S FILE • Vine leaves are a good source of calcium and are available in cans and packets. In both cases they will be packed in brine so rinse them well before using. Blanch them first in boiling water for 2 minutes, then drain and rinse in cold water, removing any stalks.

carbohydrate 17 g • protein 13 g • kJ 728 • Kcal 173

Spicy Crab and Chicken Parcels

with Sweet and Sour Dipping Sauce

175 g/6 oz white crab meat, drained if canned
125 g/4 oz cooked chicken, minced
1 garlic clove, crushed
2 spring onions, chopped
1 tablespoon chopped fresh coriander
2 teaspoons chopped preserved stem ginger, plus
2 teaspoons syrup from the jar
$1/4$ teaspoon chilli powder
1 tablespoon light soy sauce
grated rind and juice of 1 lime
8 x 10 cm/4 inch wonton wrappers
2 tablespoons olive oil, plus extra for greasing and brushing
1 spring onion, finely sliced, to garnish

Sweet and sour dipping sauce

50 g/2 oz sugar
3 tablespoons rice or wine vinegar
$1/2$ teaspoon salt
1 teaspoon dried chilli flakes
2 tablespoons water

place all the ingredients except the wonton wrappers and oil in a bowl and stir well until combined; cover and chill for 1 hour to allow the flavours to develop.

meanwhile, prepare the dipping sauce. Place all the ingredients in a small saucepan and heat gently, stirring until the sugar has dissolved. Bring to the boil and remove from the heat. Leave until cold and transfer to a small serving bowl.

brush each of the wonton wrappers with oil and place a spoonful of the crab mixture at the edge. Roll up loosely, tucking the ends in. Place on a greased baking sheet, brush the parcels with oil and bake in a preheated oven at 190°C/375°F/Gas Mark 5 for 15–20 minutes until golden and crisp. Serve the parcels hot with the dipping sauce and garnished with the spring onion.

Makes 8
Preparation time: *15 minutes, plus chilling*
Cooking time: *20–25 minutes*
Oven temperature: *190°C/375°F/Gas Mark 5*

FACT FILE • Wonton wrappers are made from wheat flour, egg and water.

carbohydrate 2 g • protein 3 g • kJ 166 • Kcal 40

Good Sources of Starch

Sources

Starchy foods, the unrefined carbohydrates, are very important for adding satisfying bulk to our diets and providing an important source of energy (calories). Starchy foods, the staples that are common to every culture, are the cheap and plentiful foods that have formed the bulk of the human diet since man first learnt to farm food. Starchy foods include bread, rice, pasta, couscous, all sorts of grains such as oats, rye, buckwheat, millet and the starchy vegetables such as potatoes, yams and plantain. Many of these foods, particularly the wholegrain cereals, are good sources of important vitamins and minerals and many of them also contribute to the protein content of the diet. Some of these vitamins will be lost in the milling process, for example rice loses its B Vitamins in the polishing process.

Quantities

Nutritionists recommend that we should all try to have a high percentage (40–50%) of the Calories we require as unrefined carbohydrates – that is starchy foods. By eating large portions of starchy foods, cooked and served with little or no fat, we can satisfy our hunger, making it easier to restrict the quantity of high fat foods we eat. A diet high in unrefined carbohydrates and fruit and vegetables, and low in fatty foods may have a protective effect against a number of diseases such as coronary heart disease and some forms of cancer.

Health

For people who are overweight a good way to reduce weight is to have a diet with a high proportion of starchy foods, but very little fat and no added sugar. Diabetics can also get good control of their blood sugar by eating this kind of diet. Eating any form of carbohydrate, sugar or starch causes a rise in blood sugar. However, starchy foods, especially the wholegrain cereals, make the blood sugar level rise quite slowly. Sugary foods cause very rapid rises in blood sugar, making the control of diabetes more difficult. The bulkiness of starchy foods gives a feeling of fullness when they are eaten and the slow release of their carbohydrate helps to sustain energy over a long period of time. For some forms of athletics, such as long distance running, a very starchy meal eaten some hours before a race has been proved to be an extremely effective way of storing energy for slow release during a long, gruelling race. The great variety of starchy food that is now available to us from all over the world can be used to add interest and variety to the diet, so that the humble starchy staple food can be quite glamorous, as well as being a very important basis for good nutrition and a healthy balanced diet.

Bread rolls

Bread

Pasta

Potatoes

Bulgar wheat

Polenta

Rice

Couscous

Spinach Pancakes
with Wild Mushrooms

Pancakes

125 g/4 oz frozen spinach, defrosted
125 g/4 oz plain flour
300 ml/¹/₂ pint skimmed milk
I egg
ground nutmeg
sunflower oil, for frying
salt and pepper
mixed salad, to serve (optional)

Filling

25 g/I oz dried cep mushrooms or
50g/2 oz chestnut mushrooms
I tablespoon olive oil
I onion, chopped
I garlic clove, chopped
250 g/8 oz button mushrooms, quartered
I tablespoon wholemeal plain flour
2 tablespoons single cream
50 g/2 oz mozzarella cheese, grated
chervil sprigs, to garnish

COOK'S FILE • The addition of a small amount of dried cep mushrooms greatly enhances the flavour of the mushroom filling. You may find them in large supermarkets labelled porcini, which is their Italian name. If unavailable use fresh chestnut mushrooms.

press the spinach to extract excess water and put it into a food processor or blender with the remaining pancake ingredients; season with salt, pepper and nutmeg to taste. Blend until smooth, then pour into a jug and leave to stand for 30 minutes.

heat a little oil in a 15 cm/6 inch non-stick frying pan. Pour a little batter into the pan. Tilt the pan to spread the batter thinly and evenly. Cook until golden underneath, then turn over and cook the other side. Repeat until all the batter has been used up. Stack the cooked pancakes on a warmed plate with rounds of greaseproof paper between them.

make the filling. Pour boiling water over the ceps, to cover and leave to soak for 15 minutes. Drain and reserve the liquid. Chop the mushrooms.

heat the oil in a frying pan and fry the onion until softened, add the garlic, button mushrooms and cep or chestnut mushrooms and cook for 2 minutes, stirring occasionally. Stir in the flour, then add 125 ml/4 fl oz of the reserved mushroom liquid or water and stir continuously until thickened. Stir in the cream and season with salt and pepper to taste.

put a tablespoon of the mushroom mixture on each pancake, roll up and place in a greased, shallow ovenproof dish. Sprinkle with the cheese and bake in a preheated oven at 190°C/375°F/Gas Mark 5 for 15 minutes until heated through. Serve with a mixed salad of cherry tomatoes and red onion, if liked, and garnished with the chervil sprigs.

Serves 4
Preparation time: *15 minutes, plus standing*
Cooking time: *40 minutes*
Oven temperature: *190°C/375°F/Gas Mark 5*

carbohydrate 38 g • protein 14 g • kJ 1354 • Kcal 323

Prawn and Monkfish Ravioli

250 g/8 oz raw prawns, peeled, deveined and finely chopped
250 g/8 oz monkfish fillet, finely chopped
2 tablespoons chopped parsley, extra to garnish
1 teaspoon grated lime rind
4 tablespoons single cream
salt and pepper
flat leaf parsley sprigs, to garnish

Pepper butter
½ large red pepper, cored and deseeded
25 g/1 oz low-fat spread
1 tablespoon lime juice

Pasta
250 g/8 oz pasta flour (or plain flour), extra for dusting
1 teaspoon salt
2 eggs, plus 1 egg yolk
1 tablespoon olive oil

to make the pepper butter, grill the pepper for 3–4 minutes on each side until charred and tender. Seal in a plastic bag until cool. Discard the skin and purée the flesh in a food processor or blender with the low-fat spread and lime juice until smooth. Season with salt and pepper to taste.

make the pasta dough. Sift the flour and salt into a bowl, and work in the eggs, egg yolk, oil and enough water to form a soft dough. Knead for 5 minutes until smooth; wrap and chill for 30 minutes.

meanwhile, make the filling. Mix the prawns and monkfish with the parsley, lime rind and cream. Season with salt and pepper and set aside.

divide the dough into 8 portions. Roll out each piece thinly on a floured surface. Take one sheet of pasta and place teaspoons of the filling at 2.5 cm/1 inch intervals on the dough. Brush lightly around the filling with water and top with a second sheet of pasta. Press down around each mound and, using a pastry cutter, stamp out the ravioli. Repeat with the remaining mixture, placing the filled ravioli on a well-floured tea towel.

add the ravioli to a large saucepan of lightly salted boiling water and boil for 3–4 minutes, then drain well. Serve with pepper butter and garnished with chopped parsley and sprigs of flat leaf parsley.

FACT FILE • To devein prawns, cut off the head and peel off the shell and legs. Score down the middle of the back to remove the dark brown intestinal vein. Wash in cold water.

Serves 4
Preparation time: *30 minutes, plus chilling*
Cooking time: *12 minutes*

carbohydrate 51 g • protein 31 g • kJ 1899 • Kcal 450

Zucchini al Forno

4 large or 8 small courgettes
1 teaspoon oil
1 garlic clove, finely chopped
500 g/1 lb canned tomatoes
50 g/2 oz canned anchovies, drained
salt and pepper

To serve
lemon slices
mixed salad

Garnish
1 teaspoon chopped thyme
1 teaspoon chopped rosemary

slice the courgettes in half lengthways, scoop out the seeds and pulp with a teaspoon. Sprinkle the inside of each courgette with salt and leave to drain upside down on absorbent kitchen paper.

heat the oil in a saucepan and lightly fry the garlic. Rub the tomatoes through a sieve to remove the seeds and add the pulp to the saucepan. Bring to the boil and cook vigorously until reduced by half. Remove from the heat and stir in one chopped anchovy fillet. Season with salt and pepper to taste.

wipe the insides of the courgettes with absorbent kitchen paper to remove the salt and set them in a large baking dish. Fill each one with some tomato sauce and arrange an anchovy fillet on top. Grind over plenty of black pepper and bake in a preheated oven at 200°C/400°F/Gas Mark 6 for about 40 minutes. Allow to cool then serve with lemon slices and salad leaves and garnished with the thyme and rosemary.

Serves 4
Preparation time: *15 minutes, plus cooling*
Cooking time: *55 minutes*
Oven temperature: *200°C/400°F/Gas Mark 6*

FACT FILE • Zucchini (courgettes) retain essential vitamins in the skin, such as K and B12, which are lost when peeled.

carbohydrate 5 g • protein 6 g • kJ 306 • Kcal 73

Vegetable Carpaccio
with Parmesan Shavings

12 small radishes, trimmed and sliced

1 green pepper, cored, deseeded and cut into thin strips

1 red pepper, cored, deseeded and cut into thin strips

2 small carrots, thinly sliced

3 celery sticks, thinly sliced

1 small fennel bulb, thinly sliced

1 tablespoon extra virgin olive oil

25 g/1 oz Parmesan cheese, shaved

pepper

divide the vegetables between 4 large plates and arrange in attractive mounds in the centre.

drizzle the vegetables with enough olive oil to lightly moisten them. Scatter the Parmesan shavings around them and garnish with a few grindings of black pepper.

Serves 4
Preparation time: *15 minutes*

FACT FILE • The main nutritional difference between old carrots and young carrots is their carotene content. Carotene is stored in the growing root, so that old carrots have a very high carotene content.

carbohydrate 3 g • protein 3 g • kJ 297 • Kcal 70

Crudités

500–600 g/1–1¼ lb assorted raw vegetables

Lentil, green peppercorn and mustard dip

25 g/1 oz green Puy lentils

2 tablespoons green peppercorns in brine, drained

2 tablespoons Dijon mustard

3 tablespoons sunflower oil

1 tablespoon lemon juice

1 tablespoon warm water

Spicy tomato salsa

1 small red onion, finely diced

1 garlic clove, finely chopped

500 g/1 lb ripe tomatoes, peeled, deseeded and diced

1–2 sweet, moderately hot red chillies, deseeded and finely chopped

3 tablespoons finely chopped coriander

1 tablespoon finely chopped parsley

2 teaspoons lime juice

2 tablespoons olive oil

pinch of salt

pinch of sugar

pinch of pepper

choose firm, crisp vegetables, such as radishes, carrots, celery, cucumber, fennel, chicory, peppers, spring onions and lettuce hearts. These can be cut into finger-length pieces or matchsticks. Tight-headed vegetables, such as broccoli or cauliflower, can be broken into florets and small whole vegetables like cherry tomatoes, mushrooms, mangetouts, green beans and radishes can be left just as they are.

wash and dry the vegetables well, then arrange them on a serving platter or individual plates.

to make the lentil, green peppercorn and mustard dip, bring a large saucepan of water to the boil, add the lentils and return to the boil. Cook for 10–15 minutes until just tender and beginning to turn mushy. Drain and refresh under cold water until completely cold.

crush the peppercorns until roughly broken using a mortar and pestle. Stir in the mustard and gradually beat in the oil, a little at a time. Stir in the lemon juice, water and cooked lentils. Pile into a serving bowl, cover and chill until required.

to make the spicy tomato salsa, put the red onion into a small bowl and cover with boiling water. Leave for a few minutes, then drain and refresh under cold water. Drain again and pat dry with absorbent kitchen paper.

combine the onion with all the remaining ingredients and mix lightly. Cover and chill for at least 30 minutes, to allow the flavours to develop.

COOK'S FILE • Tomato salsa can be varied by adding chopped olives, anchovies, capers, feta cheese or chillies and served with tortilla chips, pitta or garlic bread.

Serves 4

Preparation time: *20 minutes, plus chilling*

Cooking time: *10–15 minutes*

carbohydrate 14 g • *protein 4 g* • *kJ 844* • *Kcal 202*

Warm Broccoli Vinaigrette

375 g/12 oz broccoli
250 g/8 oz cauliflower
2 tablespoons pine nuts, toasted and chopped

Dressing
2 tablespoons tarragon vinegar
2 tablespoons coarse grain mustard
1 tablespoon olive oil
2 tablespoons very low-fat fromage frais
salt and pepper
½ red pepper, thinly sliced, to garnish

break the broccoli and cauliflower into small florets and cook in boiling salted water for 5 minutes. Drain thoroughly, put in a bowl and cover to keep warm.

to make the dressing, mix the vinegar, mustard and salt and pepper together, then gradually whisk in the oil until it thickens. Stir in the fromage frais and pour the dressing over the florets, tossing carefully until they are well coated.

arrange in individual serving bowls and sprinkle with the pine nuts. Serve garnished with red pepper strips.

Serves 4
Preparation time: *10 minutes*
Cooking time: *5 minutes*

COOK'S FILE • To retain a higher nutritional content, the broccoli and cauliflower may be steamed.

carbohydrate 5 g • *protein 9 g* • *kJ 612* • *Kcal 147*

Fish and Shellfish

Fish has always been acknowledged as a healthy option that is lower in fat than meat. It is extremely versatile with regards to both ingredients and cooking methods and tastes equally good when simply grilled or baked as it does marinated, barbecued or when included in curries, stews and pasta dishes. Here is a varied selection of fish and shellfish recipes to try, that all taste as good as they look.

Plaice
with Courgette and Lemon Sauce

8 small plaice fillets, about 65 g/2½ oz each, skinned
finely grated rind of ½ lemon
1 tablespoon finely chopped parsley
300 ml/½ pint skimmed milk
salt and pepper
lemon slices, to serve

Sauce
375 g/12 oz courgettes
300 ml/½ pint Chicken or Fish Stock (see page 10)
finely grated rind of ½ lemon
1 garlic clove, chopped

Garnish
dill sprigs
strips of lemon rind

spread out the plaice fillets, skinned sides uppermost. Season with salt and pepper, sprinkle with lemon rind and parsley, and roll each one up, securing with a cocktail stick.

make the sauce. Slice the courgettes and place them in a saucepan with the stock, lemon rind and garlic and cook until just tender. Transfer the cooked courgettes and their liquid to a blender or food processor and blend until smooth.

put the rolled plaice fillets into a deep frying pan; add the milk and season with salt and pepper. Poach the fish gently until it is just tender, about 8–10 minutes, then drain the fish, reserving the liquid. Put on a warmed serving dish.

heat the courgette purée in a saucepan with enough of the fish cooking liquid to make a fairly thin sauce. Spoon the sauce around the rolled fish fillets. Serve with lemon slices and garnished with dill sprigs and strips of lemon rind.

FACT FILE • White fish has a very low fat content, often less than 1%. The small amount of fat present is mostly mono-unsaturated or polyunsaturated. The low fat content means that white fish is also very low in Calories. Plaice, Dover sole, cod, haddock and monkfish have a particularly low fat content.

Serves 4
Preparation time: *15 minutes*
Cooking time: *15 minutes*

carbohydrate 3 g • protein 14 g • kJ 344 • Kcal 80

Poached Salmon Steaks
with Hot Basil Sauce

1 large bunch of basil
4 celery sticks, chopped
1 carrot, chopped
1 small courgette, chopped
1 small onion, chopped
6 salmon steaks, about 125 g/4 oz each
75 ml/3 fl oz dry white wine
125 ml/4 fl oz water
1 teaspoon lemon juice
15 g/¹⁄₂ oz unsalted butter
salt and pepper
lemon slices, to serve
basil leaves, to garnish

strip the leaves from half the basil and set aside. Spread all the chopped vegetables over the bottom of a large flameproof casserole dish with a lid, press the salmon steaks into the vegetables and cover them with the remaining basil. Pour over the wine and water and season with salt and pepper. Bring to the boil, cover and simmer for about 10 minutes. Transfer the salmon to a warmed serving dish.

bring the poaching liquid and vegetables back to the boil and simmer for 5 minutes. Strain into a blender or food processor and add the cooked and uncooked basil. Blend to a purée and return to a saucepan. Bring the purée to the boil and reduce by half, until thickened. Remove the saucepan from the heat, add the lemon juice and stir in the butter. Pour the sauce over the salmon steaks and serve with lemon slices and garnished with basil leaves.

FACT FILE • Salmon is a good source of Vitamin D, which we need for the absorption of calcium. The major source is the action of sunlight on the skin, and for most people dietary Vitamin D is unimportant. However, some groups such as the housebound elderly could suffer a deficiency if they do not get sufficient Vitamin D from dietary sources.

Serves 6
Preparation time: *15 minutes*
Cooking time: *25 minutes*

carbohydrate 0 g • protein 19 g • kJ 835 • Kcal 200

Grilled Cod Steaks
with Mint Pesto

4 cod steaks, about 175 g/6 oz each

olive oil, to baste

lemon juice

salt and pepper

lime wedges, to garnish

Mint pesto

6 tablespoons chopped mint

1 tablespoon chopped parsley

1 garlic clove, chopped

1 tablespoon grated Parmesan cheese

1 tablespoon single cream

1 teaspoon balsamic vinegar

3 tablespoons extra virgin olive oil

brush the cod with oil and squeeze over a little lemon juice. Season with salt and pepper and cook under a preheated moderate grill for 3–4 minutes on each side until golden and cooked through.

meanwhile, place all the ingredients for the pesto in a blender or food processor and blend until fairly smooth. Season with salt and pepper to taste and transfer to a bowl. Alternatively, pound the ingredients together with a mortar and pestle.

serve the cod steaks topped with a spoonful of the pesto and green beans, if liked. Garnish with lime wedges.

Serves 4
Preparation time: *10 minutes*
Cooking time: *about 8 minutes*

COOK'S FILE • This fragrant pesto is a particularly good partner for cod. Serve with a selection of steamed green vegetables drizzled with extra virgin olive oil and lime juice and garnished with sprigs of mint, if wished.

carbohydrate 1 g • protein 32 g • kJ 880 • Kcal 216

Sweet and Sour Cod Cutlets

4 cod cutlets or steaks, about 175 g/6 oz each

15 g/¹/₂ oz sunflower margarine

1 onion, thinly sliced

150 ml/¹/₄ pint Fish Stock (see page 11)

150 ml/¹/₄ pint orange juice

2 tablespoons wine vinegar

1 tablespoon soy sauce

2 teaspoons soft brown sugar

1¹/₂ tablespoons cornflour

Garnish

strips of orange rind

spring onion curls (see Cook's File, below)

place the pieces of cod in a deep frying pan, large enough to hold them in a single layer. Just cover with cold water and bring slowly to the boil over a moderate heat. Poach gently for about 10 minutes or until the fish is tender.

meanwhile, melt the margarine in a saucepan and sauté the onion for 5–7 minutes, until soft but not brown. Add the stock, orange juice, vinegar, soy sauce and sugar to the saucepan and stir well to combine.

blend the cornflour in a small bowl with a little water to make a creamy paste and add to the sauce. Bring to the boil, stirring, until the sauce is thickened. Simmer for 3–5 minutes.

when the fish is cooked, lift it out of the pan with a slotted spoon and place on serving plates. Pour the sauce over the fish. Serve garnished with strips of orange rind and spring onion curls.

Serves 4
Preparation time: *10 minutes*
Cooking time: *15 minutes*

COOK'S FILE • Spring onion curls are made by cutting the spring onion into thin strips and placing them in iced cold water. The longer they remain in the water, the longer the curls will last.

carbohydrate *16 g* • protein *32 g* • kJ *949* • Kcal *225*

Minerals in the Diet

Function

Our bodies need a number of minerals for health, growth and the maintenance of bones, cells and tissues. Some are only needed in very small traces, others in much larger amounts. By eating a healthy, mixed diet it is possible to get all the minerals needed every day. The more important dietary minerals are calcium, iron and zinc. Phosphorus and magnesium are also important, but a diet which provides sufficient calcium will also provide adequate phosphorus and magnesium.

Calcium

Calcium and phosphorus together form the framework of our skeleton, giving strength to bones and teeth. A deficiency of calcium in some elderly people may result in osteoporosis, where calcium is lost from the bone making it painful to bear weight. In order to prevent osteoporosis, it is important to build strong bones early in life through weight-bearing exercise and adequate dietary calcium. The best sources of dietary calcium are milk, cheese and other milk products such as yogurt. Butter and cream contain very little calcium. Calcium is often added to white bread, and soya curd products such as tofu have a high calcium content. The daily requirement of calcium is 1000 mg for males under 18 years and 700 mg for those over 19 years, 800 mg for females under 18 years and 700 mg for those over 19 years.

Iron

Iron is particularly important for the formation of haemoglobin, the red pigment in blood. In theory we are born with enough iron to last through life, but if enough dietary iron is not eaten to restore any losses, anaemia can result. The amount of iron we absorb from food is quite low, but it is increased if the body's stores are depleted or when there is a need, such as with growing children or pregnant women. The best sources of iron in the diet are meat and offal because the iron is most easily absorbed. The iron in eggs is also well absorbed but the iron in vegetables, or added to flour is less well absorbed. If a source of Vitamin C, such as orange juice or salad is included in a meal containing iron-rich vegetables such as pulses, this helps in the absorption of the iron. Tea inhibits absorption of iron, so avoid it around meal times. The daily requirement of iron for males is 11 mg for those under 18 years and 9 mg for those over 19 years; for females it is 15 mg for those under 50 years and 9 mg for those over 50 years.

Sources of Iron

Beef 50 g/2 oz
1 mg
Liver, lambs 50 g/2 oz
3.7 mg
Kidney, pigs, 50 g/2 oz
3.2 mg
Bread, white, 1 slice
0.5 mg
Bread, wholemeal, 1 slice
0.9 mg
Kidney beans, cooked, 100 g/3½ oz
1.4 mg
Lentils, cooked, 100 g/3½ oz
2.4 mg
Tofu, steamed, 100 g/3½ oz
1.2 mg
Spinach has a high iron content compared to other vegetables, but this iron may not be well absorbed.

Zinc

Zinc helps in the healing of wounds and is involved in enzyme activity. It is present in a variety of foods, but may be deficient in some diets. Zinc is associated with protein, so meat and dairy foods are good sources. The daily requirement of zinc is about 7 mg for adults and 10 mg for children.

Tofu

Milk

Cheese

Yogurt

Cereal

Pasta

Bread

Eggs

Beef

Spinach

Seafood

Beans

Swordfish Steaks
with Charmoula and Grilled Pepper Salsa

4 swordfish steaks, about 150 g/5 oz each
oil, for greasing
1 quantity of Grilled Pepper Salsa, to serve
(see page 118)
lime wedges, to garnish

Charmoula
1 teaspoon paprika
1/2 teaspoon ground turmeric
1/2 teaspoon ground cumin
2 garlic cloves, crushed
2 tablespoons chopped fresh coriander
1 tablespoon lime juice
2 tablespoons olive oil
salt and pepper

place the swordfish in a glass or ceramic dish. Combine all the charmoula ingredients together, brush over both sides of the steaks, cover and marinate for at least 4 hours, preferably overnight.

make the grilled pepper salsa according to the instructions on page 118.

cook the marinated swordfish steaks under a preheated moderately hot grill for 3–4 minutes on each side, basting them with any marinade left in the bowl, until the fish is charred and tender. Alternatively, cook over moderately hot coals on a barbecue.

serve the swordfish at once with a spoonful of grilled pepper salsa and garnished with lime wedges.

Serves 4
Preparation time: *15 minutes, plus marinating*
Cooking time: *20 minutes, including salsa*

COOK'S FILE • Swordfish is a firm-fleshed fish that is very suitable for barbecuing. Charmoula is an Arabian sauce which works equally well with tuna or halibut.

carbohydrate 4 g • protein 28 g • kJ 1075 • Kcal 258

Trout Stuffed with Couscous and Herbs

1 tablespoon olive oil

1 small onion, finely chopped

2 garlic cloves, crushed

125 g /4 oz couscous

300 ml/½ pint Fish Stock or

Vegetable Stock (see page 11)

1 tablespoon chopped parsley

1 tablespoon chopped mint

4 trout, each weighing about 300 g/10 oz, gutted, heads removed, and boned

50 g/2 oz flaked almonds (optional)

salt and pepper

warm bread, to serve (optional)

Garnish

lemon wedges

mint sprigs

heat the oil in a frying pan, add the onion and fry until softened, adding the garlic towards the end. Stir in the couscous, fish or vegetable stock, parsley and mint. Bring to the boil then remove the pan from the heat and leave for 10–15 minutes until the liquid has been absorbed.

season the trout with salt and pepper and fill the cavity of each one with a quarter of the couscous mixture. Lay the fish in a greased shallow baking dish and sprinkle over the almonds, if using. Bake in a preheated oven at 200°C/400°F/Gas Mark 6 for 15–20 minutes until the fish flakes when tested with a fork.

serve the trout with warm bread, if liked, and garnished with lemon wedges and mint sprigs.

Serves 4
Preparation time: *10 minutes*
Cooking time: *25–35 minutes*
Oven temperature: *200°C/400°F/Gas Mark 6*

FACT FILE • There are two almond varieties: the sweet almond and the bitter almond. They are mainly used dry and are rich in proteins, fats and vitamins.

carbohydrate 17 g • protein 49 g • kJ 1554 • Kcal 370

Spaghetti with Lobster

1 kg/2 lb cooked lobster, cut in half lengthways
300 g/10 oz spaghetti
2 tablespoons olive oil
2 shallots, chopped
8 plum tomatoes, skinned, deseeded and chopped
4 tablespoons lemon juice
handful of chives, chopped
salt and pepper
dried chilli flakes, to garnish

remove all the meat from the lobster and cut it into chunks.

cook the spaghetti in lightly salted boiling water, according to packet instructions.

meanwhile, heat the oil in a saucepan, add the shallots and sauté for 3 minutes. Add the tomatoes and lemon juice, season with salt and pepper and cook for a further 3 minutes.

add the lobster to the tomato sauce, stir, reduce the heat and cook for 4 minutes.

drain the pasta well and put it into a warmed serving dish. Add the sauce and the chopped chives and toss with two wooden spoons. Serve immediately, garnished with chilli flakes.

Serves 4
Preparation time: *10 minutes*
Cooking time: *15 minutes*

FACT FILE • Lobster and other shellfish are rich sources of cholesterol. Dietary cholesterol is probably not important if the total content of fat in the diet, particularly saturated fat, is not very high. Most cholesterol in the blood is made in the body from ingested fats.

carbohydrate 62 g • *protein 30 g* • *kJ 1889* • *Kcal 445*

Mediterranean Fish Stew

3 tablespoons sunflower oil

2 onions, sliced

2 carrots, sliced

3 celery sticks, sliced

125 g/4 oz mushrooms, sliced

2 garlic cloves, crushed

4 tomatoes, skinned and chopped

300 ml/½ pint dry white wine

600 ml/1 pint Fish Stock or
Vegetable Stock (see page 11)

1 bay leaf

750 g/1½ lb cod or haddock fillet, skinned and boned

200 g/7 oz jar mussels in brine, drained

175 g/6 oz peeled prawns

salt and pepper

chopped parsley, to garnish

heat the oil in a large saucepan and add the onions, carrots, celery, mushrooms and garlic. Cook until softened, but not brown. Add the tomatoes, wine, stock and bay leaf. Season with salt and pepper to taste and simmer for 15 minutes.

cut the fish into 5 cm/2 inch cubes. Add them to the saucepan and simmer for 15 minutes.

add the mussels and prawns and simmer for 2–3 minutes.

to serve, turn the stew into a warmed serving dish and garnish with the chopped parsley.

Serves 6
Preparation time: *15 minutes*
Cooking time: *40 minutes*

COOK'S FILE • If you add wine, beer or other alcoholic drinks to dishes which are then cooked at a fairly high temperature, the alcohol content of the drink will evaporate. The wine, beer or cider will impart flavour to the dish but no alcohol. The Calorie content of wine and other alcoholic drinks comes mostly from alcohol, so the cooking process will eliminate these calories.

carbohydrate 6 g • protein 33 g • kJ 1087 • Kcal 259

Prawn, Mango and Mozzarella Salad

with Grilled Pepper Salsa

125 g/4 oz salad leaves
25 g/1 oz radicchio, shredded
1 large ripe mango, peeled, stoned and thinly sliced
1 tablespoon extra virgin olive oil
150 g/5 oz mozzarella cheese, sliced
12 large cooked peeled prawns

Grilled Pepper Salsa
1 large red pepper
1/2 tablespoon balsamic vinegar
pinch of sugar
1 tablespoon extra virgin olive oil, plus extra for
brushing
salt and pepper

start by making the grilled pepper salsa. Brush the pepper with a little oil and cook under a preheated hot grill for 10–12 minutes, turning frequently until charred all over. Place the pepper in a plastic bag, seal and set aside until cool enough to handle.

skin and deseed the pepper over a bowl to catch the juices, then roughly chop the flesh. Place it in a blender or food processor with the juices, vinegar and sugar and blend until smooth. Transfer to a bowl and whisk in the oil, season with salt and pepper to taste and set aside.

arrange the salad leaves and radicchio on a plate with the mango slices fanned out and the mozzarella slices and the prawns in the middle. Drizzle over the grilled pepper salsa and a little olive oil. Serve garnished with black pepper.

Serves 4
Preparation time: *15 minutes*
Cooking time: *10–12 minutes*

FACT FILE • Mango is a rich source of iron and Vitamin A. It also contains some of the Vitamins B and C.

carbohydrate 9 g • protein 13 g • kJ 894 • Kcal 214

Seafood Risotto

1 litre/1¾ pints hot Fish Stock (see page 11)

25 g/1 oz butter

2 tablespoons olive oil

3 shallots, chopped

1 garlic clove, crushed and chopped

300 g/10 oz arborio or canaroli rice

375 g/12 oz peeled raw prawns, tails left on

2 tablespoons roughly chopped parsley

75 ml/3 fl oz white wine or vermouth

25 g/1 oz Parmesan cheese, freshly grated

salt and pepper

Garnish

bay leaves

2 tablespoons chopped parsley

heat the stock in a saucepan to a gentle simmer. Melt half the butter and 1 tablespoon of the olive oil in another saucepan, add the shallots and garlic and sauté for 5 minutes until softened but not brown.

add the rice and stir well to coat the grains thoroughly with the butter and oil. Pour in enough hot stock to cover the rice, stir well and simmer gently. Continue stirring as frequently as possible throughout the cooking. As the liquid is absorbed, add more stock by the ladle to just cover the rice, and stir well.

when half of the stock has been incorporated, add the prawns, turn the heat up a little and continue to add the stock by the ladle; stir carefully so as not to break up the seafood.

when all the stock has been absorbed, add the parsley, the remaining butter, white wine or vermouth, half of the Parmesan, and season with salt and pepper to taste. Stir well. Serve garnished with the remaining Parmesan, the bay leaves and the chopped parsley.

Serves 4
Preparation time: *15 minutes*
Cooking time: *35 minutes*

FACT FILE • Risotto literally means 'little rice' in Italian and can be served as a side dish, or as a main course if prepared with fish or chicken.

carbohydrate 63 g • protein 27 g • kJ 2109 • Kcal 505

Meat and Poultry

Meat and poultry provide many essential vitamins and minerals as well as providing the basis for substantial meals. The selection of dishes in this chapter combines simplicity with creativity to provide a modern feel. The recipes are suitable for all occasions and can be combined with one of the salad or vegetable dishes in the later chapters.

Garlic Chicken
with Lemon Sauce

4 boneless, skinless chicken breasts
2 tablespoons lemon juice
1 tablespoon sunflower oil
mangetout, to serve (optional)

Stuffing
125 g/4 oz curd cheese or quark
2 garlic cloves, finely chopped
1 tablespoon chopped thyme
1 tablespoon chopped rosemary
pepper

Sauce
25 g/1 oz sunflower margarine
25 g/1 oz plain flour
300 ml/¹/₂ pint hot Chicken Stock (see page 10)
2 tablespoons lemon juice
salt and pepper

Garnish
lemon slices
rosemary sprigs

place the chicken breasts between sheets of greaseproof paper and flatten with a rolling pin. Place in a large, shallow dish in a single layer. Mix the lemon juice and oil together and pour over the chicken breasts. Leave to marinate for 15 minutes, turning once or twice.

to make the stuffing, mix all the ingredients together in a bowl. Lift the chicken breasts out of the marinade with a slotted spoon. Reserve the marinade. Spread the stuffing over the chicken breasts, roll them up and secure with wooden cocktail sticks.

brush the marinade over the chicken breasts and cook under a preheated moderate grill for 10–15 minutes on each side, brushing them with more marinade as they cook.

meanwhile, make the sauce. Melt the margarine in a small saucepan over a moderate heat. Stir in the flour and cook for 1 minute. Remove the saucepan from the heat and gradually add the stock, stirring well. Return to the heat and bring to the boil, stirring continuously. Allow to boil for 1 or 2 minutes. Add the lemon juice and heat through. Season with salt and pepper.

thinly slice the chicken breasts when cooked and arrange on warmed serving plates. Serve with mangetout, if liked. Pour over the sauce and garnish with lemon slices and rosemary sprigs.

COOK'S FILE • This dish is delicious served with a green vegetable such as mangetout and boiled new potatoes.

Serves 4
Preparation time: *15 minutes, plus marinating*
Cooking time: *20–30 minutes*

carbohydrate 6 g • *protein 38 g* • *kJ 1209* • *Kcal 288*

Pimento Chicken

2 kg/4 lb oven-ready chicken
1 onion, quartered
1 carrot, sliced
2 celery sticks, sliced
4 juniper berries, crushed
1 bay leaf
4–6 parsley stalks
salt
6 peppercorns, lightly crushed
griddled courgette slices, to serve (optional)
chopped parsley, to garnish

Sauce

250 g/8 oz canned pimentos, drained, rinsed and chopped
1 tablespoon tomato purée
2 tablespoons mango chutney
200 ml/7 fl oz low-fat natural yogurt
salt and pepper

put the chicken, vegetables, juniper berries, bay leaf, parsley, salt and peppercorns into a saucepan. Cover with water. Bring to the boil, cover the saucepan and simmer for $1^{1}/_{2}$–2 hours, or until the chicken is tender. Leave the chicken to cool in the stock. Lift out the chicken, drain and dry it. Reserve the stock, discarding the bay leaf. Skin the chicken and slice the meat from the bones.

to make the sauce, put the pimentos, 2 tablespoons of the reserved chicken stock, tomato purée and chutney into a saucepan and bring to the boil. Transfer to a blender or food processor and blend until smooth. Set aside to cool. Blend the cooled pimento mixture with the yogurt and season with salt and pepper to taste.

arrange the chicken on a warmed serving dish and pour over the sauce. Serve with griddled courgettes, if liked and garnished with the parsley.

Serves 8
Preparation time: *15 minutes, plus cooling*
Cooking time: $1^{3}/_{4}$–$2^{1}/_{4}$ *hours*

FACT FILE • Pimentos are small sweet peppers, used as a garnish and often as a stuffing in olives. They can be bought fresh, pickled or bottled in brine. Use fresh red pepper if you cannot find pimento.

carbohydrate 7 g • *protein 38 g* • *kJ 1145* • *Kcal 273*

Chicken *with Ginger*

375 g/12 oz boneless, skinless chicken breasts

1 tablespoon dry sherry

4 spring onions, chopped

2 large carrots, thinly sliced

2.5 cm/1 inch piece of fresh root ginger, peeled and finely chopped

1 tablespoon oil

1–2 garlic cloves, thinly sliced

2 celery sticks, diagonally sliced

1 small green pepper, cored, deseeded and sliced

1 small yellow pepper, cored, deseeded and sliced

2 tablespoons light soy sauce

2 tablespoons lemon juice

grated rind of 2 lemons

1/2 teaspoon chilli powder

chives, to garnish

cut the chicken into 7 cm/3 inch strips. Combine the sherry, spring onions, carrots and ginger, add the chicken and toss well to coat, then set aside for 15 minutes.

heat the oil in a large non-stick frying pan or wok. Add the garlic, celery and green and yellow peppers and stir-fry for 1 minute. Add the chicken and marinade and cook for 3 minutes. Stir in the soy sauce, lemon juice and rind and chilli powder and cook for a further 1 minute.

divide between 4 warmed serving plates, and serve immediately, garnished with chives.

Serves 4
Preparation time: *20 minutes, plus marinating*
Cooking time: *4–5 minutes*

FACT FILE • Ginger can be bought fresh or dried. The fresh variety does not keep well, but if kept, it should be wrapped in foil and stored in the refrigerator. The dry variety has a much longer shelf life, but should be kept in an airtight container.

carbohydrate 3 g • *protein 21 g* • *kJ 624* • *Kcal 148*

Grilled Chicken
Sala Thai Style

8 chicken drumsticks, skinned
2 tablespoons crushed garlic
2 tablespoons chopped fresh coriander root or stem
1/2 teaspoon pepper
1 teaspoon salt
2 tablespoons dark soy sauce
3 tablespoons honey
2 teaspoons ground ginger
1 tablespoon oyster sauce
boiled rice, to serve (optional)

Garnish
1/2 large red chilli, thinly sliced
2 spring onions, sliced into strips
2 teaspoons toasted sesame seeds

pierce the chicken drumsticks with a fork.

put the crushed garlic, chopped coriander root or stem and the pepper into a blender or food processor and blend to a paste. Alternatively, pound together using a mortar and pestle.

place the garlic mixture and the remaining ingredients in a dish large enough to hold the chicken drumsticks in a single layer. Coat the chicken well in the marinade, cover and set aside for 2 hours.

grill the marinated drumsticks under a preheated, medium hot grill or on a barbecue for 20–30 minutes, turning frequently, until cooked through. Serve with boiled rice, if liked, and garnished with the chilli, spring onions and toasted sesame seeds.

Serves 4
Preparation time: *15 minutes, plus marinating*
Cooking time: *20–30 minutes*

FACT FILE • Chicken skin can be desirable in a dish as it provides a great deal of flavour and helps prevent the chicken from drying out during cooking. The downside is that skin is made almost entirely from fats of different kinds.

carbohydrate 13 g • *protein 17 g* • *kJ 683* • *Kcal 162*

All about Fat

Fat in the diet

Fat adds richness and moistness to food and improves the taste. We need some fat, for energy and its content of fat-soluble vitamins. However, all fats are very concentrated sources of energy (Calories) and excess consumption causes weight gain. A high concentration of fat in the diet may also increase the risk of coronary heart disease and some forms of cancer. It is advisable to restrict the total amount of fat in the diet, to maintain a healthy weight and control the level of cholesterol in the blood.

Cholesterol

This is a natural and necessary substance made in the body from dietary fats, but high levels of blood cholesterol are linked to coronary heart disease. There are two kinds of fat present in the blood, triglycerides and cholesterol. High levels of triglyceride can be reduced by restricting alcohol intake and eating a diet high in soluble fibre. High levels of cholesterol may be reduced by restricting fat in the diet, and changing the type of fat that is eaten.

What kind of fat?

The chief sources of fat in the diet are dairy products, meat, oils and fried foods. Fatty fish such as trout and mackerel contain fish oils, which are valuable in the diet. However, some foods may be high sources of hidden fats, for example biscuits, cakes, pastries. Fats can be divided into three classes, saturated, monounsaturated and polyunsaturated.

Saturated fats

These are usually solid at room temperature. Examples include butter, lard, meat fat and cheese. The process of hardening vegetable oil to make margarine changes the fat content to a higher proportion of saturated fat. A high intake of saturated fat raises blood cholesterol, particularly the fraction of cholesterol that is thought to be the most harmful, the low-density lipoproteins.

Monounsaturated fats

It has been observed that where a population eats most of their fat as olive oil, there is a low incidence of coronary heart disease. It is now thought that mono-unsaturated fats are protective against coronary heart disease. A high proportion of these oils helps to lower cholesterol in the blood and maintain the important high-density lipoproteins. Good sources are olive oil and rapeseed oil.

Polyunsaturated fats

These help decrease the cholesterol level in blood. Good sources are vegetable oils, such as sunflower, safflower and corn oils.

Butter and margarine

It is important to remember that butter and margarine have the same Calorie (energy) content, whether or not the margarine is marked 'polyunsaturated'. Butter is a good source of the fat-soluble Vitamins A and D, and these vitamins are added to margarine.

Low-fat spreads

All these have a high water content and therefore a lower Calorie content than margarine or butter. Low-fat spreads usually have added fat-soluble vitamins.

Cheese and cream

Most cheeses have a high fat content, however, lower fat varieties of some hard cheeses are available. Many soft cheeses can be bought in low-fat varieties. Quark is very low in fat, and low-fat ricotta or fromage frais are also good. Double cream is 50% fat, but for a treat, use whipping cream instead.

Fish

Double cream

Single cream

Butter

Olive oil

Sunflower oil

Cheese

Nuts

Yogurt

Margarine

Quark

Penne *with Chicken Livers*

1 yellow pepper, cored and deseeded
300 g/10 oz penne
1 tablespoon olive oil
25 g/1 oz butter
1 red onion, sliced
250 g/8 oz chicken livers, trimmed
1 rosemary sprig, chopped
salt and pepper
25 g/1 oz Parmesan cheese, grated, to serve

roast the yellow pepper in a hot oven or under a preheated hot grill, skin-side up, until the skin is blistered and black. Place in a plastic bag and allow to cool, then peel off the skin. Cut the flesh into strips.

cook the penne in lightly salted boiling water, according to packet instructions.

meanwhile, heat the oil and butter in a large frying pan, add the sliced onion and chicken livers and cook over a high heat until browned all over. Add the rosemary, the yellow pepper strips and season with salt and pepper. Do not overcook the livers as they will become dry and hard: they are best when still pink in the middle.

mix the chicken liver mixture with the cooked pasta and toss well. Serve immediately with the Parmesan.

Serves 4
Preparation time: *10 minutes*
Cooking time: *10–15 minutes*

FACT FILE • Liver is a particularly rich source of Vitamins A and D, because this is the main storage site for amounts over the normal requirement. Vitamins A and D are both important in the diet, but should not be eaten in excess. Very high levels of Vitamin A are dangerous in pregnancy.

carbohydrate 62 g • *protein 25 g* • *kJ 1969* • *Kcal 467*

Sweet and Sour Chinese Turkey

500 g/1 lb boneless, skinless turkey breast
2 tablespoons lemon juice
5 tablespoons orange juice
4 celery sticks
2 sharon fruit or firm tomatoes
8–10 radishes
1/2 Chinese cabbage
1 large green pepper, cored and deseeded
2 tablespoons oil
150 ml/1/4 pint Chicken Stock (see page 10)
1 1/2 teaspoons cornflour
1 tablespoon soy sauce
1 tablespoon clear honey
boiled rice, to serve (optional)
orange rind, to garnish

cut the turkey breast into thin strips. Marinate in the lemon and orange juices for 30 minutes. Cut the celery, sharon fruit or tomatoes, radishes, Chinese cabbage and green pepper into small neat pieces.

heat the oil in a large non-stick frying pan or wok. Drain the turkey and reserve the marinade. Fry the turkey in the oil until nearly cooked. Add the vegetables and sharon fruit or tomatoes and heat for 2–3 minutes.

blend the chicken stock with the marinade and the cornflour. Add the soy sauce and honey. Pour this mixture over the ingredients in the pan and stir until thickened. Serve immediately with boiled rice, if liked, and garnished with orange rind.

Serves 4
Preparation time: *15 minutes, plus marinating*
Cooking time: *8 minutes*

FACT FILE • Sharon fruit is a variety of persimmon and can be eaten like an apple. The fruit can be peeled, but the skin is also edible.

carbohydrate 17 g • protein 29 g • kJ 1030 • Kcal 245

Griddled and Roast Guinea Fowl

1.75 kg/3½ lb guinea fowl, jointed into 8 pieces
2 tablespoons Dijon mustard
grated rind and juice of 2 lemons
1 teaspoon vegetable oil
sea salt flakes and pepper
griddled sweet potato slices, to serve (optional)
strips of lemon rind, to garnish

heat a griddle pan until hot, put on the guinea fowl joints and cook for about 6 minutes on each side. The skin should be quite charred to give the guinea fowl a good flavour.

mix the Dijon mustard, lemon rind and juice together and season with salt and pepper.

remove the guinea fowl from the pan and place in a lightly oiled roasting tin. Using a pastry brush, brush the joints with the mustard mixture, then cook on the top shelf of a preheated oven at 200°C/400°F/Gas Mark 6 for 20 minutes. To test, insert a sharp knife into the thickest part of each joint – when cooked, the juices should run clear.

serve the guinea fowl with griddled slices of sweet potato, if liked, and garnished with the lemon rind.

Serves 4
Preparation time: *10 minutes*
Cooking time: *about 40 minutes*
Oven temperature: *200°C/400°F/Gas Mark 6*

FACT FILE • Mustard pastes are easy to make and add taste and texture to poultry dishes. Griddling helps to form a crust, and finishing the cooking process in the oven ensures that the meat is properly cooked throughout.

carbohydrate 1 g • protein 39 g • kJ 1064 • Kcal 254

Chinese Pork
with Bamboo Shoots

2 tablespoons groundnut oil
300 g/10 oz lean pork, shredded
1 small Chinese cabbage, shredded
1 tablespoon coarsely chopped hazelnuts
250 g/8 oz canned bamboo shoots, drained with
juices reserved, and sliced
2 tablespoons soy sauce
1 teaspoon curry powder
pinch of chilli powder
small pinch of sugar
salt and pepper
soy sauce, to serve (optional)

heat the oil in a non-stick frying pan or wok, add the pork and stir-fry quickly until lightly browned. Season with salt and pepper. Add the cabbage, hazelnuts and a few tablespoons of the liquid from the can of bamboo shoots. Cook, stirring, for about 5 minutes.

add the bamboo shoots, reserving some to garnish, soy sauce, curry powder, chilli powder and sugar, mixing well. Cook gently for a further 10 minutes. Serve immediately, with soy sauce if liked, and garnished with the reserved bamboo shoots.

Serves 4
Preparation time: *15 minutes*
Cooking time: *20 minutes*

FACT FILE • Stir-frying is a healthy, low-fat cooking method, as the design of the wok ensures that heat is evenly spread and the food cooks more quickly. Less oil is required when stir-frying and the quick cooking time means that more of the vitamins are retained.

carbohydrate 6 g • protein 19 g • kJ 913 • Kcal 219

Orecchiette

with Spicy Tomato and Pancetta Sauce

1 tablespoon olive oil
1 onion, chopped
2 garlic cloves, chopped
75 g/3 oz pancetta
400 g/13 oz can chopped tomatoes
½–1 teaspoon crushed dried chillies
125 ml/4 fl oz red wine
300 g/10 oz orecchiette
handful of flat leaf parsley, chopped
handful of basil, chopped
salt and pepper

Garnish

whole red chillies
basil leaves

heat the olive oil in a saucepan, add the onion, garlic and pancetta and sauté for 5 minutes.

add the tomatoes, chillies and red wine and simmer for 15 minutes, or until the sauce is rich and thick.

meanwhile, cook the pasta in lightly salted boiling water, according to packet instructions. Drain well.

stir the parsley and basil into the sauce and season with salt and pepper to taste. Add the sauce to the pasta and toss well. Serve, garnished with red chillies and basil leaves.

Serves 4
Preparation time: *5 minutes*
Cooking time: *20 minutes*

FACT FILE • Pancetta is pork belly, cured with salt and spices and rolled into a sausage shape.

carbohydrate 62 g • protein 16 g • kJ 1860 • Kcal 440

Lamb *with Piquant Sauce*

8 lamb cutlets, trimmed
8 tablespoons Worcestershire sauce
2 beef stock cubes
2 teaspoons chopped rosemary
1 teaspoon ground coriander
125 ml/4 fl oz water
salt and pepper
rosemary sprigs, to garnish

To serve
boiled rice (optional)
mangetout (optional)

put the lamb cutlets in a flameproof dish. Put the Worcestershire sauce in a small bowl, crumble in the stock cubes and stir in the rosemary and coriander. Pour over the lamb and leave to marinate for at least 3 hours, turning frequently.

remove the lamb from the marinade and cook under a preheated hot grill for 10 minutes, or until the lamb is cooked to your taste. Turn the meat frequently, spooning over some of the marinade to prevent burning.

put the remaining marinade in a saucepan with the water, salt and pepper, and bring to the boil. Arrange the lamb cutlets on warmed serving plates. Pour over the sauce and serve with boiled rice and mangetout, if liked, and garnished with rosemary sprigs.

Serves 4
Preparation time: *15 minutes, plus marinating*
Cooking time: *10–15 minutes*

FACT FILE • Mangetout literally means 'eat it all' in French and this is the case as the seeds in this peapod hardly develop, so the whole pod is eaten.

carbohydrate 5 g • *protein 28 g* • *kJ 1071* • *Kcal 242*

Stir-Fried Garlic Lamb

375 g/12 oz lamb fillet
2 tablespoons dry sherry
2 tablespoons light soy sauce
1 tablespoon dark soy sauce
1 teaspoon sesame oil
1 tablespoon groundnut or sunflower oil
6 garlic cloves, thinly sliced
1 cm/½ inch piece of fresh root ginger, peeled and finely chopped
1 leek, thinly sliced diagonally
4 spring onions, chopped
rice noodles, to serve (optional)
spring onion strips, to garnish

cut the lamb into thin slices across the grain. Combine the sherry, soy sauces and sesame oil, add the lamb and toss until well coated. Leave to marinate for 15 minutes, then drain, reserving the marinade.

heat the oil in a non-stick frying pan or wok, add the meat and about 2 teaspoons of the marinade and fry briskly for about 2 minutes, until well browned. Add the garlic, ginger, leek and spring onions and fry for a further 3 minutes.

transfer to warmed serving bowls and serve immediately, on a bed of rice noodles, if liked, and garnished with the spring onion strips.

Serves 4
Preparation time: *15 minutes, plus marinating*
Cooking time: *5 minutes*

FACT FILE • Light soy sauce is distinctly lighter in colour than traditional soy sauce. The colour of soy sauce is dependent upon the length of time that it has been aged.

carbohydrate 2 g • *protein 20 g* • *kJ 823* • *Kcal 197*

Spinach-stuffed Lamb

250 g/8 oz spinach, cooked, drained and chopped
15 g/½ oz mint, finely chopped
4 garlic cloves, finely chopped
1 teaspoon vinegar
pinch of sugar
½ small leg of lamb (knuckle end), boned
175 ml/6 fl oz red wine
salt and pepper

To serve

salad leaves (optional)
shredded carrot (optional)

mix the spinach with the mint, garlic, vinegar and sugar and season with salt and pepper.

trim every scrap of fat from the lamb. Lay it flat with the boned side up and spread over the spinach mixture. Fold over the meat and secure with string as if tying a parcel. Place the meat in a roasting dish or tin and pour over the red wine, adding a little water if the tin is much larger than the meat. Cook in a preheated oven at 180°C/350°F/Gas Mark 4 for 45–55 minutes, depending on how well done you like lamb.

transfer to a hot carving platter and cut into thick slices. Pour off the excess fat from the roasting tin and pour the remaining juices around the lamb slices. Serve with salad leaves and shredded carrot, if liked.

Serves 4
Preparation time: *20 minutes*
Cooking time: *45–55 minutes*
Oven temperature: *180°C/350°F/Gas Mark 4*

FACT FILE • It is best to ask your butcher to remove the bone from the leg of lamb, but not to roll it. The piece of meat should be roughly triangular.

carbohydrate 3 g • *protein 28 g* • *kJ 897* • *Kcal 214*

Stir-fried Beef
with Peppers

1 tablespoon olive oil
1 onion, thinly sliced
1 large garlic clove, cut into thin strips
500 g/1 lb fillet steak, cut into thin strips
1 red pepper, cored, deseeded and cut into
matchsticks
1 green pepper, cored, deseeded and cut into
matchsticks
1 tablespoon soy sauce
2 tablespoons dry sherry
1 tablespoon chopped rosemary
salt and pepper
brown rice, to serve (optional)

heat the olive oil in a non-stick frying pan or wok and stir-fry the onion and garlic for 2 minutes. Add the strips of beef and stir-fry briskly until evenly browned on all sides and almost tender.

add the peppers and stir-fry for a further 2 minutes. Add the soy sauce, sherry, salt and pepper, and the rosemary, and stir-fry for a further 1–2 minutes.

serve immediately with brown rice, if liked.

Serves 4
Preparation time: *15 minutes*
Cooking time: *about 10 minutes*

COOK'S FILE • Fillet steak is the best cut to use for this dish. Less expensive cuts tend to be tougher and are better suited to slower methods of cooking.

carbohydrate 7 g • protein 24 g • kJ 860 • Kcal 205

Spicy Beef Koftas
in Pizzaiola Sauce

1 tablespoon sunflower or olive oil
1 large onion, finely chopped
2 garlic cloves, crushed
1 red chilli, deseeded and finely chopped
2 red peppers, cored, deseeded and chopped
400 g/13 oz can plum tomatoes
300 ml/½ pint Vegetable Stock (see page 11)
2 tablespoons double concentrate tomato purée
2 tablespoons finely chopped basil
1 teaspoon finely chopped oregano
pinch of sugar
1 tablespoon chopped flat leaf parsley
50–125 g/2–4 oz black Kalamata olives, pitted
flat leaf parsley sprigs, to garnish

Koftas
1 medium egg
50 g/2 oz coarse breadcrumbs
500 g/1 lb lean minced beef
75 g/3 oz onion, grated
2 tablespoons plain flour
1 tablespoon sunflower or olive oil
salt and pepper
boiled rice, to serve (optional)

first make the koftas. Beat the egg in a large bowl, stir in the breadcrumbs and add the beef and onion. Season with salt and pepper. Work the ingredients together until well combined. You will find that your hands are best for this. Divide the mixture into 8 portions, shape each one into a ball and roll in a little flour. Heat the oil in a large frying pan and fry the koftas until evenly browned, turning frequently. This will take about 10 minutes.

meanwhile, prepare the sauce. Heat the oil in a saucepan and fry the onion and garlic until soft but not brown. Add the remaining ingredients, except half of the olives. Bring to the boil and cook over a high heat for 10 minutes to concentrate the flavours and slightly reduce the liquid.

using a slotted spoon, lower the koftas into the sauce. Cover and cook gently for about 30 minutes until the meat is cooked through and the sauce is rich and pulpy. Remove about 50 ml/2 fl oz of the sauce and a few olives and process to a thick purée in a food processor or blender. Stir into the sauce. Season with salt and pepper to taste. Serve with rice, if liked, and garnished with the parsley sprigs and remaining olives.

Serves 4
Preparation time: *20 minutes*
Cooking time: *1 hour*

FACT FILE • Koftas originate from central and northern India. As well as fried, koftas can be grilled.

carbohydrate 29 g • protein 33 g • kJ 1587 • Kcal 378

Hot Thai Beef Salad

2 ripe papayas, peeled and thinly sliced

1/2 large cucumber, cut into matchsticks

75 g/3 oz bean sprouts

1 medium head crisp lettuce, shredded

2 tablespoons vegetable oil

500 g/1 lb rump or fillet steak, cut into thin strips across the grain

3 garlic cloves, finely chopped

2 green chillies, thinly sliced

8 tablespoons lemon juice

1 tablespoon Thai fish sauce (*nam pla*)

2 teaspoons sugar

arrange the papaya, cucumber, bean sprouts and lettuce in individual piles on a large serving platter. Cover loosely and set aside.

heat the oil in a heavy-based frying pan or wok over a moderate heat until hot. Add the beef, garlic and chillies, increase the heat to high and stir-fry for 3–4 minutes or until browned on all sides. Pour in the lemon juice and fish sauce, add the sugar and stir-fry until sizzling.

remove the wok from the heat. Remove the beef from the dressing with a slotted spoon and divide between 4 plates on a bed of bean sprouts and lettuce, arranging the papaya to one side and the cucumber and spring onion on the top. Pour over the dressing and serve immediately.

Serves 4
Preparation time: *15 minutes*
Cooking time: *5 minutes*

FACT FILE • Bean sprouts contain most of the vitamins of the B complex and if eaten in large enough quantities will provide useful amounts of them. The B Vitamins are water-soluble, and riboflavin, or Vitamin B2 is destroyed by light. Keep vegetables cool and in a dark place. Milk contains riboflavin, so glass bottles should not be kept in the light.

carbohydrate 16 g • protein 28 g • kJ 1174 • Kcal 280

Vegetarian Main Courses

It is no longer just the vegetarian who opts for the meat-free meal. Many people enjoy the variety of vegetarian food that is now available and the colours and textures that are created. The recipes selected here are no exception, as freshly prepared vegetables are combined with beans, pulses, pasta, couscous and rice, to provide a delicious selection of healthy dishes that everyone can enjoy.

Tomato and Vegetable Lasagne

2 tablespoons olive oil

2 onions, sliced

1 small celery head, chopped

250 g/8 oz mushrooms, quartered

1 small aubergine, sliced

750 g/1½ lb canned tomatoes

125 g/4 oz runner beans, trimmed and roughly chopped

1 bay leaf

1 teaspoon caster sugar

175 g/6 oz quick-cook lasagne verde

300 g/10 oz low-fat natural yogurt

125 g/4 oz reduced-fat Edam cheese, grated

pinch of cayenne pepper

½ teaspoon mustard powder

salt and pepper

heat the oil in a large saucepan and cook the onions and celery over a moderate heat for about 5 minutes until they are beginning to soften. Add the mushrooms and aubergine. When all the fat has been absorbed, pour in the tomatoes and runner beans and bring to the boil. Add the bay leaf and sugar. Season with salt and pepper to taste and boil uncovered for 25 minutes.

pour one third of the vegetable mixture into a 1.8 litre/3 pint ovenproof dish. Cover with a layer of uncooked lasagne. Repeat twice more.

mix the yogurt with the cheese, cayenne pepper and mustard. Spread the mixture over the lasagne.

cook the lasagne in a preheated oven at 180°C/350°F/Gas Mark 4 for 1 hour. Serve immediately.

Serves 6
Preparation time: *10 minutes*
Cooking time: *1½ hours*
Oven temperature: *180°C/350°F/Gas Mark 4*

COOK'S FILE • This lasagne can be served as a family meal with a fresh green salad and crusty French bread.

carbohydrate *41 g* • protein *17 g* • kJ *1332* • Kcal *316*

Fettuccine
with Walnut Sauce

250 g/8 oz fettuccine
1 tablespoon olive oil
50 g/2 oz walnuts
bunch of chives
175 g/6 oz fat-free fromage frais
25 g/1 oz Parmesan cheese, grated
salt
chive flowers, to garnish

cook the pasta in lightly salted boiling water, according to packet instructions. Drain thoroughly, rinse well, drain again, toss in oil, then transfer to a warmed serving dish and keep warm.

put the walnuts and chives into a blender or food processor and chop finely. Alternatively, chop finely with a knife and mix together.

to make the sauce, put the fromage frais into a heavy-based saucepan and heat very gently, taking care not to let it boil. Stir in the Parmesan, and the walnut and chive mixture and heat through gently. Pour the sauce over the pasta and garnish with chive flowers.

Serves 4
Preparation time: *10 minutes*
Cooking time: *15 minutes*

FACT FILE • Walnuts have a very high fat content, but nearly half of this is polyunsaturated. Pecan nuts are sometimes used instead of walnuts and have a similar fat content. In pecan nuts, however, there is less polyunsaturated and more monounsaturated fat.

carbohydrate 45 g • protein 16 g • kJ 1549 • Kcal 368

Penne

with Broad Beans, Asparagus and Mint

300 g/10 oz penne

500 g/1 lb asparagus, trimmed and cut into
5 cm/2 inch lengths

2 tablespoons olive oil

250 g/8 oz broad beans or peas

75 ml/3 fl oz half-fat crème fraîche

50 g/2 oz Parmesan cheese, grated, plus extra
to garnish

4 tablespoons chopped mint, plus extra
to garnish

salt and pepper

cook the pasta in lightly salted boiling water, according to packet instructions.

meanwhile, steam the asparagus for 10–12 minutes. Alternatively, place on a baking sheet, brush with olive oil and place under a preheated hot grill for 8 minutes, turning as the pieces brown.

cook the broad beans or peas in lightly salted boiling water for 2 minutes, or until tender.

drain the pasta. Pour the crème fraîche into the empty pasta pan over the heat, add the beans or peas, the asparagus and the Parmesan. Heat gently and season with salt and pepper to taste. Return the pasta to the pan, add the mint and toss well with two wooden spoons. Serve immediately, garnished with Parmesan and mint.

FACT FILE • Broad beans contain soluble and insoluble fibre and protein. Combining a pulse vegetable with a grain-based food such as pasta improves the efficiency of the protein in the dish. Such dishes are important sources of protein for vegetarians.

Serves 4
Preparation time: *10 minutes*
Cooking time: *20 minutes*

carbohydrate 66 g • *protein 23 g* • *kJ 2009* • *Kcal 477*

Stir-fried Noodles

with Broccoli, Sweetcorn, Bean Sprouts and Smoked Tofu

175 g/6 oz dried thread egg noodles

sunflower oil, for deep-frying

250 g/8 oz firm smoked tofu, cubed

1 onion, finely chopped

1 teaspoon grated fresh root ginger

2 garlic cloves, crushed

1 small red chilli, deseeded and finely sliced

250 g/8 oz broccoli florets

175 g/6 oz baby sweetcorn, cut in half lengthways

175 g/6 oz fresh bean sprouts

2 red chillies, deseeded and cut in half, to garnish

Sauce

250 ml/8 fl oz teriyaki sauce

2 tablespoons sake (Japanese rice wine)

2 tablespoons lemon juice

2–3 teaspoons sweet chilli sauce

2 teaspoons brown sugar

FACT FILE • Tofu is a curd made from soya beans and is a good protein source for vegetarians. It has a similar protein content to pulses and can be a rich source of calcium, depending on the method used to make it.

cook the noodles in a large saucepan of boiling water according to packet instructions until just tender. Drain and refresh under cold running water until very cold. Leave to drain.

heat about 5 cm/2 inches sunflower oil in a heavy-based frying pan or wok and fry the tofu cubes for 3–4 minutes until crisp and lightly golden. Drain on kitchen paper and keep warm. Remove all but a few tablespoons of the oil from the wok and fry the onion, ginger, garlic and chilli until soft but not brown. Remove from the heat.

blanch the broccoli in a large saucepan of boiling water for about 1 minute, drain and refresh under cold water. Drain again and pat dry with kitchen paper. Combine all the ingredients for the sauce in a bowl and mix well.

return the frying pan or wok with the onion mixture to the heat. When reheated, add the broccoli and stir-fry for 2–3 minutes. Add the sweetcorn and bean sprouts and stir-fry for about 3 minutes. Add the sauce, toss to combine, then add the noodles and the fried tofu. Cook for another 1 minute until heated through. Serve garnished with chilli halves.

Serves 4
Preparation time: *20 minutes*
Cooking time: *20 minutes*

carbohydrate 49 g • *protein 21 g* • *kJ 1574* • *Kcal 374*

Hot Spiced Stew
with Potatoes and Cauliflower

375 g/12 oz whole lentils or split yellow peas, rinsed
and soaked in water for 15 minutes

1.8 litres/3 pints Vegetable Stock (see page 11)

3 tablespoons vegetable oil

2 large onions, cut into wedges

1–1.25 kg/2–2¹/₂ lb potatoes, cut into chunks

1 cauliflower, cut into florets and stalks removed

3–4 garlic cloves, crushed

2 teaspoons turmeric

2 tablespoons black mustard seeds

1–2 tablespoons fennel seeds

1–2 small green chillies, deseeded and chopped

1 teaspoon saffron threads, soaked in 2 tablespoons
warm water

125 g/4 oz coconut cream

2 tablespoons chopped coriander

salt and pepper

rinse the lentils or split peas under cold running water, drain and put into a large saucepan with half of the stock. Bring to the boil, then reduce the heat and simmer for 30 minutes until the lentils or split peas are soft and all the liquid has been absorbed.

meanwhile, prepare and cook the vegetables. Heat the oil in a large saucepan, add the onions and fry over a low heat for about 8 minutes, stirring frequently. Add the potatoes and cauliflower to the pan with the garlic and cook for 1 minute. Stir in the turmeric, mustard and fennel seeds and the chopped chillies, mixing them in the pan. Add the remaining stock and the soaked saffron threads and bring to the boil. Reduce the heat and cook gently for 10–15 minutes or until the vegetables are almost cooked.

when the lentils or split peas are cooked, mash them with a potato masher to form a thick purée, leaving a few whole. Add the coconut cream and stir well to mix. Add this thick purée to the vegetables and stir well to combine. This will make the stew rich and thick. Season with salt and pepper and cook gently until the vegetables are completely tender and the flavours combined. Stir in the coriander and serve immediately.

FACT FILE • The fat content of different makes of coconut cream available in the supermarket varies enormously, from about 22% to 68%. For healthier eating, choose the lower fat varieties. Although it is a vegetable, the fat content of coconut is almost entirely saturated.

Serves 6
Preparation time: *15 minutes, plus soaking*
Cooking time: *45 minutes*

carbohydrate 70 g • *protein 24 g* • *kJ 2052* • *Kcal 487*

Courgette and Bean Provençale

175 g/6 oz cannellini beans, soaked overnight
3 tablespoons olive oil
2 onions, sliced
2 garlic cloves, chopped
500 g/1 lb courgettes, diced
400 g/13 oz can chopped tomatoes
2 tablespoons tomato purée
2 teaspoons chopped oregano
1 bouquet garni
50 g/2 oz black olives, halved and pitted
salt and pepper
oregano sprigs and leaves, to garnish

drain the beans, put them in a large saucepan, cover with fresh water and bring to the boil. Cover and simmer for 45 minutes–1 hour until almost tender, adding salt towards the end of the cooking time. Drain, reserving 150 ml/¼ pint of the cooking liquid.

heat the oil in the saucepan and fry the onions until soft but not browned. Add the garlic and courgettes and fry gently, stirring occasionally, for a further 15 minutes.

add the tomatoes, tomato purée, oregano, bouquet garni, salt and pepper, the drained beans and reserved liquid. Cover and simmer gently for 20 minutes, adding the olives 5 minutes before the end of the cooking time. Serve immediately, garnished with oregano sprigs and leaves.

Serves 4
Preparation time: *15 minutes, plus soaking*
Cooking time: *about 1 hour 20 minutes*

FACT FILE • Oregano has a pungent flavour and is popular in Mediterranean dishes. The flavour becomes much stronger when it is dried and should be used more sparingly.

carbohydrate 35 g • protein 16 g • kJ 1254 • Kcal 300

Bean Tagine

500 g/1 lb red or white kidney beans,
soaked overnight

2 celery sticks, halved

2 bay leaves

4 parsley sprigs

4 tablespoons olive oil

500 g/1 lb onions, chopped

5 garlic cloves, crushed

2 red chillies, deseeded and chopped

4 red peppers, cored, deseeded and chopped

1 tablespoon paprika

large handful of mixed chopped mint,
parsley and coriander

salt and pepper

mint leaves, to garnish

Sauce

1 kg/2 lb canned chopped tomatoes

2 tablespoons olive oil

4 parsley sprigs

1 tablespoon sugar

drain the beans and boil in fresh, unsalted water for 10 minutes, then drain. Tie the celery, bay leaves and parsley together with kitchen string. Cover the beans with fresh unsalted water, add the celery and herbs and simmer for about 1 hour until the beans are just tender. Drain, reserving the cooking liquid, and discard the celery and herbs.

meanwhile, make the sauce. Empty the tomatoes and their juice into a saucepan, add the oil, parsley and sugar and bring to the boil then simmer, uncovered, for about 20 minutes until thick.

heat the oil in a heavy flameproof casserole. Add the onions, garlic, chillies, red peppers and paprika and cook gently for 5 minutes. Stir in the beans, the sauce and enough of the reserved cooking liquid to just cover the beans. Season with salt and pepper, cover and cook in a preheated oven at 150°C/300°F/Gas Mark 2 for 1½ hours, stirring occasionally.

just before serving, stir in the mint, parsley and coriander. Serve immediately, garnished with mint leaves.

Serves 8
Preparation time: *30 minutes, plus soaking*
Cooking time: *2¾ hours*
Oven temperature: *150°C/300°F/Gas Mark 2*

FACT FILE • Pulses contain a mixture of soluble and insoluble fibre. In red kidney beans the ratio of soluble to insoluble fibre is about two to one. Soluble fibre lowers blood cholesterol.

carbohydrate 41 g • protein 17 g • kJ 1285 • Kcal 305

Asparagus and White Wine Risotto

1.5 litres/2¹/₂ pints Vegetable Stock (see page 11) or water

500 g/1 lb young asparagus, trimmed, with trimmings reserved

1 bay leaf

2 large onions, 1 quartered and 1 finely chopped

50 g/2 oz unsalted butter

475 g/15 oz arborio rice

300 ml/¹/₂ pint dry white wine

25 g/1 oz Parmesan cheese, grated

salt and pepper

sprigs of basil, to garnish

bring the stock or water to the boil, add the asparagus trimmings, the bay leaf and onion quarters and boil for 20 minutes. Strain into another saucepan and return the stock to the boil.

cut the asparagus tips into 4 cm/1½ inch lengths. Cut half of the stems into similar lengths and chop the rest finely, reserving a few spears to serve. Cook the tips and stems in the stock for 3–4 minutes, until just tender. Lift all the asparagus from the stock, drain and refresh under cold running water. Drain and reserve. Keep the stock simmering.

melt half of the butter in a large heavy-based saucepan over a low heat. Add the chopped onion and cook very gently until soft but not brown. Stir in the rice and cook, stirring constantly, until the rice is opaque. Add the wine and boil for 1 minute, stirring all the time. Add a ladleful of simmering stock and stir until it is absorbed, then repeat the process until nearly all the stock has been absorbed and the rice is almost cooked. Stir constantly to prevent the rice sticking.

add all the asparagus with the remaining stock and cook until the asparagus is tender and the rice creamy. Stir in the remaining butter and season with salt and pepper. Serve, topped with grated Parmesan and asparagus spears and garnished with basil sprigs.

FACT FILE • Asparagus has a low energy (Calorie) value and a high content of Vitamins A and C.

Serves 4
Preparation time: *20 minutes*
Cooking time: *1 hour*

carbohydrate 121 g • protein 16 g • kJ 2931 • Kcal 695

Lentil Moussaka

3 tablespoons vegetable oil

I onion, chopped

4 celery sticks, chopped

I garlic clove, crushed

400 g/13 oz can chopped tomatoes

250 g/8 oz green lentils

2 tablespoons Japanese soy sauce

900 ml/1 1/2 pints water

500 g/1 lb aubergines, sliced

salt and pepper

I tablespoon grated Parmesan cheese

I tablespoon oregano, to garnish

Topping

2 eggs, beaten

150 ml/1/4 pint low-fat fromage frais

heat 1 tablespoon of the oil in a saucepan, add the onion and cook until softened. Add the celery, garlic, tomatoes with their juice, lentils, soy sauce, 1/4 teaspoon pepper and water. Cover and simmer for 50 minutes, until cooked.

heat the remaining oil in a griddle pan, add the aubergine slices in batches and cook on both sides until golden. Alternatively, cook under a preheated moderate grill.

cover the base of a shallow ovenproof dish with the lentil mixture and arrange a layer of aubergine slices on top. Repeat the layers, finishing with a layer of aubergine slices.

mix the topping ingredients, season with salt and pepper to taste, and pour over the aubergines. Top with the cheese and bake in a preheated moderate oven at 180°C/350°F/Gas Mark 4 for 30–40 minutes, until golden. Serve garnished with oregano.

Serves 4
Preparation time: *20 minutes*
Cooking time: *1 1/4 –1 1/2 hours*
Oven temperature: *180°C/350°F/Gas Mark 4*

FACT FILE • Lentils are a useful source of iron in the vegetarian diet. Iron from vegetable sources is not as easily absorbed as iron from animal sources. However, a source of Vitamin C (salad, peppers, fruit juice) taken at the same time aids the absorption of vegetable iron.

carbohydrate 43 g • protein 25 g • kJ 1603 • Kcal 380

Vegetable Couscous

2 tablespoons olive oil

2 onions, sliced

1 teaspoon ground cinnamon

1 teaspoon turmeric

1 teaspoon ground ginger

$^1/_2$ teaspoon chilli powder

2 garlic cloves, crushed

2 carrots, diced

125 g/4 oz broad beans

475 g/15 oz canned chickpeas, drained

2 tablespoons tomato purée

600 ml/1 pint Vegetable Stock (see page 11)

375 g/12 oz couscous

50 g/2 oz raisins

2 courgettes, sliced

125 g/4 oz green beans, cut into 2.5 cm/1 inch lengths

2 whole canned tomatoes, cut into 8 pieces

2 tablespoons chopped parsley

2 tablespoons blanched almonds, toasted

salt and pepper

chopped parsley and parsley sprigs

heat the oil in a large saucepan, over which you can later fit a steamer. Add the onions to the saucepan and fry gently until softened. Add the spices and garlic and cook for 1 minute.

add the carrots, broad beans, chickpeas and tomato purée with the stock, bring to the boil, season with salt and pepper to taste and cook for 20 minutes.

meanwhile, put the couscous into a bowl, cover with water and leave to soak for 15 minutes. Drain thoroughly, mix in the raisins and put into a steamer or colander, lined with muslin.

add the courgettes, green beans, tomatoes and parsley to the vegetables and stir well. Fit the steamer or colander over the saucepan, making sure the bottom does not touch the stew. Steam, uncovered, for 20 minutes, until the vegetables are tender and the couscous is heated through.

turn the couscous on to a large, round serving dish and separate the grains with a fork. Ladle on a little broth to moisten it, and shape into a mound. Lift out the vegetables, place over the mound of couscous and sprinkle with the almonds. Serve garnished with sprigs of parsley and chopped parsley.

FACT FILE • Couscous is a hard wheat semolina which has been ground, dampened and rolled in flour. It is widely used in North African countries and has given its name to a dish composed of the couscous grain and a delicious vegetable stew which accompanies it.

Serves 4
Preparation time: *15 minutes, plus soaking*
Cooking time: *50 minutes*

carbohydrate 80 g • protein 17 g • kJ 1947 • Kcal 460

Breton Beans

with Cheese and Herb Crust

3 tablespoons olive oil

2 large onions, finely sliced

2–3 garlic cloves, chopped

2 large courgettes, cut into 1 cm/¹/₂ inch dice

2 red peppers, cored, deseeded and diced

2 x 400 g/13 oz cans chopped tomatoes

1 tablespoon double concentrate tomato purée

2 x 400 g/13 oz cans butter or other white beans, drained

150 ml/¹/₄ pint Vegetable Stock (see page 11)

1 tablespoon finely chopped parsley

2 bay leaves

1 teaspoon sugar

salt and pepper

salad leaves, to serve (optional)

parsley, to garnish

Cheese and Herb Crust

1 small French stick, very thinly sliced

2 tablespoons olive oil

2 tablespoons finely chopped basil

1 tablespoon finely chopped parsley

50 g/2 oz Parmesan cheese, finely grated

heat the oil in a large saucepan or flameproof casserole dish and fry the onions and garlic until soft but not brown. Add the courgettes and continue to fry for a few minutes until beginning to brown. Add all the remaining ingredients, except salt, and stir well to combine. Bring to the boil, reduce the heat, cover and simmer until the tomatoes are thick and pulpy and the flavours blended. This will take about 30–40 minutes. Taste and adjust the seasoning, adding salt if necessary.

uncover the stew. Brush the bread slices with oil, arrange on top of the stew and scatter with the herbs and Parmesan. Toast under a preheated grill until the bread is golden brown and crisp. Serve immediately with mixed salad leaves, if liked, and garnished with parsley.

Serves 6
Preparation time: *15 minutes*
Cooking time: *1 hour*

FACT FILE • Courgettes are low in Calories and, if tender, it is not necessary to peel them. They are best eaten steamed or cooked in their own juice, as boiling reduces their flavour.

carbohydrate 69 g • protein 21 g • kJ 2018 • Kcal 479

Sweetcorn & Red Pepper Frittata

2–3 tablespoons light olive oil
1 onion, finely chopped
2 garlic cloves, crushed
1 celery stick, finely chopped
1 red pepper, cored, deseeded and finely diced
5 large eggs
2 tablespoons milk
200 g/7 oz canned sweetcorn, drained
3 tablespoons finely chopped parsley
2–3 tablespoons fine white breadcrumbs
4 tablespoons grated Parmesan cheese
2 level teaspoons unsalted butter
salt and pepper
rocket leaves, to garnish

heat the oil in a frying pan and fry the onion, garlic and celery until soft but not brown. Stir in the red pepper and continue to cook until soft and beginning to brown. Set aside to cool.

break the eggs into a bowl and mix with the milk until just blended, using a fork. Transfer the cooked vegetables to the eggs with a slotted spoon, leaving behind any excess oil. Stir in the sweetcorn, parsley, breadcrumbs and half of the Parmesan. Season well with salt and pepper.

put the butter into a 15 cm/6 inch omelette pan and heat until foaming but not brown. Pour the frittata mixture into the pan, stirring with a fork while pouring to disperse the vegetables. The pan will be almost full. Stop stirring, turn the heat down to very low and cook for about 5–10 minutes. The eggs should be set with only the top surface runny.

sprinkle the remaining Parmesan on top of the frittata and slide the pan under a preheated grill for about 1 minute, just long enough to set the top and brown the cheese slightly. Leave to rest for a few minutes before sliding out on to a board or plate and cutting into wedges, fingers or cubes. Serve garnished with rocket leaves.

Serves 4
Preparation time: *15 minutes*
Cooking time: *15–20 minutes*

FACT FILE • Sweetcorn is a maize vegetable, which has been improved over the years to be used in domestic cooking.

carbohydrate 24 g • protein 14 g • kJ 1150 • Kcal 275

Salads and Vegetables

Fresh salads and vegetables are the epitome of healthy eating. The combinations are endless and with a little imagination a sensational selection of salads and side dishes can be created to accompany main courses or as a light alternative.

Mushroom Salad

275 g/9 oz button mushrooms

juice of ½ lemon

2 tablespoons sliced gherkins

175 g/6 oz tomatoes, skinned, deseeded and finely chopped

1 garlic clove, crushed

1 parsley sprig, finely chopped

pinch of sugar

2 tablespoons olive oil

salt and pepper

trim the mushroom stalks level with the caps. Put the mushrooms into a sieve, rinse and drain thoroughly. Cut into thin slices, put into a bowl and sprinkle with the lemon juice. Add the gherkins and tomatoes and mix well to blend.

to make the dressing, beat the garlic with the parsley, salt and pepper to taste, sugar and oil. Pour over the mushroom salad and toss well to combine. Leave to marinate in the refrigerator for 10–15 minutes to allow the flavours to develop. Serve lightly chilled.

Serves 4

Preparation time: *15 minutes, plus marinating*

FACT FILE • This piquant salad makes a delicious accompaniment to cold roast chicken. It can also be served as a starter or packed into a plastic box for a picnic.

carbohydrate 2 g • *protein 2 g* • *kJ 280* • *Kcal 68*

Courgette and Mixed Leaf Salad

4 tablespoons light French dressing
1 garlic clove, crushed
275 g/9 oz courgettes, thinly sliced
500 g/1 lb salad leaves
50 g/2 oz green or black olives, halved and pitted
1 tablespoon pine nuts
salt and pepper

put the French dressing and garlic into a salad bowl. Add the sliced courgettes and toss well. Leave to stand for 30 minutes to allow the courgettes to absorb the flavour of the dressing.

tear the salad leaves into manageable pieces and add to the courgettes and dressing with the olives and pine nuts. Season with salt and pepper to taste. Toss the salad thoroughly before serving.

Serves 6
Preparation time: *15 minutes, plus standing*

FACT FILE • Pine nuts are high in protein and have long been used in Italian and French dishes.

carbohydrate 2 g • *protein 2 g* • *kJ 283* • *Kcal 69*

Marinated Courgette and Bean Salad

250 g/8 oz green beans

375 g/12 oz courgettes, diced

475 g/15 oz canned blackeye beans, drained

2 tablespoons olive oil

2 tablespoons lemon juice

1 garlic clove, crushed

2 tablespoons chopped parsley

salt and pepper

crusty bread, sliced and toasted, to serve (optional)

cut the beans into 2.5 cm/1 inch lengths and cook in lightly salted boiling water for 5 minutes. Add the courgettes and cook for a further 5 minutes. Drain thoroughly and place in a bowl with the blackeye beans.

add the remaining ingredients, with salt and pepper to taste, while still warm and mix well to combine. Leave to cool and serve with toasted slices of crusty bread, if liked.

Serves 4
Preparation time: *10 minutes, plus cooling*
Cooking time: *10 minutes*

FACT FILE • Blackeye beans have a high nutritional value and contain soluble dietary fibre, which helps to control the level of cholesterol in the blood.

carbohydrate 25 g • protein 12 g • kJ 870 • Kcal 207

Oriental Pasta Salad

oil, see method

300 g/10 oz caserecce twists or other dried pasta

150 g/5 oz mangetout, trimmed

125 g/4 oz asparagus tips, halved widthways

1 large carrot, cut into 2.5 cm/1 inch matchsticks

4 spring onions, cut into 2.5 cm/1 inch matchsticks

2 red peppers, cored, deseeded and cut into

2.5 cm/1 inch matchsticks

2 tablespoons sesame oil

2 tablespoons sunflower oil

2.5 cm/1 inch piece of fresh root ginger, peeled and finely shredded

2 teaspoons sesame seeds

50 ml/2 fl oz soy sauce

salt and pepper

cook the pasta in plenty of boiling salted water, with a dash of oil for 8–12 minutes until just tender. Drain the pasta, rinse in a colander under cold running water and drain again. Transfer to a bowl.

blanch the mangetout and asparagus in a saucepan of boiling water for 2 minutes, then drain and rinse in a colander under cold running water and drain again. Add to the bowl of pasta with the carrot, spring onions and red peppers.

heat the sesame and sunflower oils in a small heavy-based saucepan. Add the ginger and sesame seeds and cook for 30–60 seconds until they start to pop. Remove the pan from the heat, stir in the soy sauce, and season with salt and pepper, to taste.

pour the dressing over the pasta and mix thoroughly.

Serves 4
Preparation time: *10 minutes*
Cooking time: *8–12 minutes*

FACT FILE • Sesame seeds and sesame oil contain an almost equal amount of polyunsaturated and monounsaturated fat. Sesame seeds have a high calcium content, but in the quantities eaten this is probably not a significant source of calcium in the average diet.

carbohydrate 65 g • *protein 14 g* • *kJ 1578* • *Kcal 373*

Potato, Celery and Apple Salad

500 g/1 lb new potatoes
2 crisp dessert apples
1 tablespoon lemon juice
1 celery head, thinly sliced
125 g/4 oz half-fat Cheddar cheese, diced
1 red onion, thinly sliced
2 tablespoons wine vinegar
2 tablespoons apple juice
1 teaspoon mild French mustard
pinch of sugar
3 tablespoons sunflower oil
salt and pepper
sprigs of dill or chervil, to garnish

cook the potatoes in lightly salted boiling water for 20–25 minutes until just tender. Drain. As soon as the potatoes can be comfortably handled, peel off the skins. The skins may be left on, if preferred. When the potatoes are quite cool, cut them carefully into 5 mm/¼ inch slices.

remove the cores from the apples and cut them into thin segments. Sprinkle with a little of the lemon juice. Mix together the potatoes, apples, celery, cheese and onion. In a small bowl, beat together the remaining lemon juice, vinegar, apple juice, mustard, sugar and oil. Season with salt and pepper to taste. Pour the dressing over the potato mixture and mix thoroughly.

place the salad in serving bowls and serve garnished with sprigs of dill or chervil.

Serves 6
Preparation time: *20 minutes, plus cooling*
Cooking time: *20–25 minutes*

FACT FILE • The vitamins in root vegetables are mainly contained just under the skin, so to ensure the highest vitamin content, these vegetables can be carefully washed instead of peeled.

carbohydrate 19 g • *protein 7 g* • *kJ 738* • *Kcal 170*

FAT ♥   IRON ■

Bean and Rice Salad

75 g/3 oz red kidney beans
50 g/2 oz cannellini beans
175 g/6 oz brown rice
2 spring onions, finely chopped
50 g/2 oz raisins
50 g/2 oz cashew nuts, roasted
½ red pepper, cut into diamonds
2 tablespoons chopped parsley
salt and pepper
lemon wedges, to serve
sprigs of flat leaf parsley, to garnish

Dressing
75 ml/3 fl oz sunflower oil
2 tablespoons soy sauce
1 tablespoon lemon juice
1 garlic clove, crushed

soak the kidney beans and cannellini beans separately in cold water overnight.

drain the beans and place them separately in 2 large saucepans. Cover with plenty of cold water, bring to the boil over a high heat and boil for 15 minutes. Reduce the heat, cover and simmer for 1–1½ hours, adding a little salt towards the end. Drain and cool.

meanwhile, cook the rice in plenty of lightly salted boiling water for 40–45 minutes until tender. Rinse, drain well and cool.

place the beans and rice in a large mixing bowl and stir in the onions, raisins, nuts, red pepper and parsley. Season with salt and pepper to taste.

place all the dressing ingredients in a screwtop jar and shake until well blended. Season with salt and pepper. Pour over the rice and bean mixture and stir well.

transfer to serving plates and serve with lemon wedges, and garnished with parsley sprigs.

FACT FILE • Rice is one of the least nutritious grains, containing little protein and no fat. However brown rice, in which the husk and embryo remain, contains B Vitamins, which is important for cultures dependent on rice as their main energy source. Brown rice provides a small amount of insoluble fibre.

Serves 6
Preparation time: *10 minutes, plus soaking*
Cooking time: *1¼–1¾ hours*

carbohydrate 42 g • *protein 9 g* • *kJ 1285* • *Kcal 366*

Spring Cabbage and Pepper Salad

4 tablespoons light French dressing
1 teaspoon light soy sauce
250 g/8 oz spring cabbage, shredded
3 celery sticks, sliced
4 spring onions, chopped
1 red pepper, cored, deseeded and diced
diced red pepper and pepper strips, to garnish

combine the dressing with the soy sauce. Put the spring cabbage in a bowl with the dressing, mix thoroughly and leave to marinate for 1 hour.

add the remaining ingredients and mix thoroughly. Serve, garnished with diced pepper and pepper strips.

Serves 6
Preparation time: *15 minutes, plus marinating*

FACT FILE • Spring cabbage is an unusual ingredient for a salad. Pick over the leaves carefully, discarding any that are blemished. Make this salad the same day as you buy the spring cabbage, as the leaves soon become limp.

carbohydrate 4 g • protein 1 g • kJ 257 • Kcal 61

Balsamic Braised Leeks and Peppers

2 tablespoons olive oil

2 leeks, cut into 1 cm/½ inch pieces

1 orange pepper, cored, deseeded and cut into 1 cm/½ inch chunks

1 red pepper, cored, deseeded and cut into 1 cm/½ inch chunks

3 tablespoons balsamic vinegar

handful of flat leaf parsley, chopped

salt and pepper

heat the olive oil in a saucepan, add the leeks and peppers and stir well, then cover the pan and cook gently for 10 minutes.

add the balsamic vinegar and cook for a further 10 minutes without a lid. The vegetables should be brown from the vinegar and all their liquid should have evaporated.

season well with salt and pepper and stir in the chopped parsley just before serving.

Serves 4
Preparation time: *5 minutes*
Cooking time: *20 minutes*

FACT FILE • Balsamic vinegar is a richly flavoured dark-coloured vinegar, made from unfermented Trebbiano grapes. It is an Italian speciality from Modena and the surrounding area.

carbohydrate 6 g • *protein 2 g* • *kJ 340* • *Kcal 82*

Fricassée of Mushrooms

50 g/2 oz unsalted butter

I large onion, finely chopped

2 garlic cloves, finely chopped

I kg/2 lb mixed wild mushrooms

2 tablespoons finely chopped parsley

175 ml/6 fl oz red wine

I egg yolk

I teaspoon arrowroot

4 tablespoons low-fat single cream

2 tablespoons finely snipped chives

salt and pepper

crème frâiche, to serve

chives, to garnish

melt the butter in a large frying pan and fry the onion and garlic until soft but not brown. Add the mushrooms and cover with a lid or sheet of foil. Cook over a gentle heat for about 10 minutes to draw out the juices – at this stage the mushrooms should stew rather than fry.

add the parsley and red wine to the mushrooms. Bring to the boil, then cook gently over a low heat for a few minutes. Blend the egg yolk with the arrowroot and cream and use to thicken the wine and mushroom juices. Stir in the chives and season with salt and pepper.

arrange the mushroom fricassée in warmed serving bowls. Serve immediately, with a spoonful of crème frâiche and garnished with chives.

Serves 4
Preparation time: *10 minutes*
Cooking time: *25 minutes*

FACT FILE • Crème fraîche is obtained from pasteurized cows' milk, to which bacteria culture is added to give it a distinctive flavour.

carbohydrate 8 g • *protein 8 g* • *kJ 946* • *Kcal 228*

Stir-fried Chinese Cabbage

8–10 Chinese cabbage leaves
2 tablespoons oil
125 g/4 oz canned bamboo shoots, drained and
sliced
1 onion, sliced
1 celery stick, sliced
lemon juice
salt and pepper
lemon slices, to garnish

cut the Chinese cabbage leaves diagonally into thin strips.

heat the oil in a non-stick frying pan or wok. Add all the vegetables and fry gently for about 8 minutes, stirring frequently. Add a little lemon juice and season with salt and pepper to taste. Garnish with lemon slices and serve.

Serves 4
Preparation time: *10 minutes*
Cooking time: *8 minutes*

FACT FILE • Chinese cabbage is a delicately flavoured vegetable of the cabbage family that originated in eastern Asia several hundred years ago.

carbohydrate 7 g • *protein 2 g* • *kJ 376* • *Kcal 90*

Fruit and Vegetables

Sources

Fruit and vegetables are good sources of vitamins and other nutrients and provide fibre in the diet. This fibre may help to reduce cholesterol and there is also evidence to suggest that eating plenty of fruit and vegetables may help to protect against some forms of cancer. Many fruits and vegetables are good sources of the antioxidant vitamins, Vitamin C, Vitamin E and B-carotene, and scientists recommend that we should increase our intake (excluding potatoes) to at least five servings daily.

Storage

It is important to preserve the vitamin content of fruit and vegetables by careful storage. Choose the freshest produce and eat soon after purchase. Some B Vitamins, such as folic acid, found in green leafy vegetables, are sensitive to light, so keep vegetables cool and in a dark place.

Cooking

Start cooking all vegetables with boiling water, or steam them quickly. Eat vegetables just after cooking and do not leave them to stand. Frozen fruit and vegetables may be just as high in vitamins as fresh vegetables, so use these as well.

Servings

The following are examples of one serving of fruit or vegetables.

COOKED VEGETABLES
2 tablespoons

SALAD
1 dessert bowl
GRAPEFRUIT/AVOCADO
½ fruit
APPLE, BANANA, ORANGE OR OTHER CITRUS FRUITS
1 fruit
PLUM/SMALL FRUITS
2 fruits
GRAPES, CHERRIES, BERRIES
1 cupful
FRESH FRUIT SALAD, STEWED OR CANNED FRUIT
2–3 tablespoons
DRIED FRUIT
½–1 tablespoon
FRUIT JUICE
1 glass (150 ml/¼ pint)

Vitamin C

The recommended daily Vitamin C intake for adults in the United Kingdom is 40 mg. Some countries have higher recommendations, and others lower. Below is a list of selected foods and their Vitamin C contents.

BLACKCURRANTS, COOKED, 125 g/4 oz
150 mg
GREEN PEPPERS 125 g/4 oz
100 mg
ORANGES, RAW, 1 SMALL
50 mg
TOMATOES, 1 SMALL
10 mg

Potatoes

Most of the Vitamin C in potatoes is close to the skin, so either serve potatoes in their skins, or peel them carefully to retain the vitamins. Cooking technique is also important, as potatoes and other vegetables will lose less of their vitamin content if they are steamed, rather than boiled.

Broccoli

Red pepper

Green pepper

Aubergine

Cabbage

Cauliflower

Apple

Pear

Banana

Mixed salad

Papaya

Orange

Pink grapefruit

Passion fruit

Blackcurrants

Kiwi fruit

Cabbage, Beetroot and Apple Sauté

40 g/1½ oz butter

½ red cabbage, thinly shredded

1 tablespoon chopped thyme

2 teaspoons caraway seeds

1 teaspoon ground mixed spice

1 tablespoon sugar

150 ml/¼ pint red wine

2 tablespoons port

2 tablespoons red wine vinegar

2 dessert apples

250 g/8 oz cooked beetroot, cubed

50 g/2 oz pecan nuts, toasted

salt and pepper

melt 25 g/1 oz of the butter in a large frying pan and fry the cabbage, thyme, caraway seeds, mixed spice and sugar for 10 minutes. Add the wine, port and vinegar and bring to the boil. Cover the pan and cook over a low heat for 20 minutes.

meanwhile, quarter, core and thickly slice the apples. Melt the remaining butter in a clean frying pan and fry the apples for 4–5 minutes until lightly golden. Add to the cabbage with the pan juices and the beetroot. Cover and cook for a further 15–20 minutes until the cabbage is tender. Season with salt and pepper, to taste. Stir in the pecan nuts and serve immediately.

Serves 4
Preparation time: *20 minutes*
Cooking time: about *55 minutes*

FACT FILE • In comparison with green cabbage both red and white cabbage have a low content of carotene (pre-vitamin A). The Vitamin E content of red and white cabbage is also lower than that of the outer leaves of green cabbage.

carbohydrate 20 g • protein 5 g • kJ 1027 • Kcal 247

Aubergine, Tomato and Mozzarella Mountains

I aubergine, cut into 8 slices

2 beef tomatoes, skinned, then cut into 8 slices

175 g/6 oz buffalo mozzarella cheese, cut into 8 slices

I tablespoon olive oil

salt and pepper

4 tablespoons green pesto, to serve

mint sprigs, to garnish

arrange the aubergine slices under a preheated hot grill and cook until browned on both sides.

place 4 of the aubergine slices on a greased baking sheet. Put a tomato slice and a mozzarella slice on each one, then make a second layer of aubergine, tomato and mozzarella, sprinkling them with salt and pepper as you go. Skewer each stack with a cocktail stick to hold them together.

place the stacks in a preheated oven at 190°C/375°F/Gas Mark 5 and cook for 10 minutes.

transfer the stacks to individual serving plates and remove the cocktail sticks. Drizzle with a little olive oil and top with a generous spoonful of pesto. Serve warm or at room temperature, garnished with mint sprigs.

Serves 4
Preparation time: *10 minutes*
Cooking time: *20 minutes*
Oven temperature: *190°C/375°F/Gas Mark 5*

COOK'S FILE • As well as making a delicious side dish, this recipe could be a light meal if served with a green salad.

carbohydrate 6 g • *protein 14 g* • *kJ 895* • *Kcal 214*

Persian Noodles

600 ml/1 pint Chicken Stock (see page 10) or
Vegetable Stock (see page 11)
125 g/4 oz noodles
1 large aubergine, cut into bite-sized pieces
4 courgettes, sliced
1 teaspoon ground mace
salt and pepper
flat leaf parsley, to garnish

place the stock in a large saucepan and bring to the boil. Add the noodles and cook for 5 minutes, then add the aubergine, courgettes and mace. Season with salt and pepper to taste.

reduce the heat and cook for a further 10–15 minutes, or until the noodles and vegetables are tender. Adjust the seasoning to taste, then drain and divide between 4 serving dishes. Serve immediately, garnished with flat leaf parsley.

Serves 4
Preparation time: *10 minutes*
Cooking time: *about 20 minutes*

FACT FILE • Mace is a spice that is obtained from the skin of the nutmeg. It has a more subtle flavour than nutmeg.

carbohydrate 23 g • protein 5 g • kJ 530 • Kcal 126

Saffron-spiced Vegetable Couscous

475 g/15 oz couscous

250 g/8 oz carrots, cut into 1.5 cm/³/₄ inch chunks

250 g/8 oz turnips, cut into 1.5 cm/³/₄ inch chunks

1–2 large fennel bulbs, each cut into 6 wedges

1 large aubergine, cut into 1.5 cm/³/₄ inch cubes

250 g/8 oz courgettes, cut into 1.5 cm/³/₄ inch slices

25 g/1 oz butter

2–3 tablespoons finely chopped coriander

salt

coriander sprigs, to garnish

Sweet Spicy Sauce

2 tablespoons extra virgin olive oil

2 large onions, cut into wedges

4 garlic cloves, crushed

2.5 cm/1 inch piece of fresh root ginger, grated

1 tablespoon ground cumin

1 tablespoon ground coriander

1 teaspoon turmeric

1 teaspoon paprika

1 teaspoon black pepper

5 cm/2 inch cinnamon stick

1 teaspoon saffron threads, soaked in 2 tablespoons warm water

750 ml/1¼ pints Vegetable Stock (see page 11)

2 x 400 g/13 oz cans chopped tomatoes

2 tablespoons tomato purée

2 tablespoons sweet chilli sauce

put the couscous into a bowl, cover with 300 ml/½ pint of water and leave to soak for 10 minutes. Fork through and leave for 10 minutes.

meanwhile, prepare the sauce. Heat 1 tablespoon of the oil in a large saucepan. Fry the onions until beginning to brown, then add the garlic and ginger. Stir in the ground spices and cinnamon stick and fry for a few minutes. Add the soaked saffron to the pan with the stock, tomatoes, tomato purée and chilli sauce. Bring to the boil. Add the carrots and turnips to the sauce, reduce the heat, cover and cook for about 10 minutes.

heat the remaining oil in a large frying pan and fry the fennel wedges until lightly coloured. Transfer to the sauce with a slotted spoon. Fry the aubergine and courgettes until browned, adding a little extra oil if necessary. Drain and add to the sauce. Cook gently for 15–20 minutes until the vegetables are tender and the sauce is rich and thick. During this final cooking, steam the couscous according to packet instructions.

to serve, pile the couscous in a large dish, fleck with pieces of butter and stir in with a fork. Stir the chopped coriander into the stew and season with salt to taste. Serve a mound of couscous to each person, spoon the vegetable stew on top and garnish with coriander sprigs.

Serves 6
Preparation time: *20 minutes, plus soaking*
Cooking time: *about 1 hour*

carbohydrate 85 g • protein 14 g • kJ 2094 • Kcal 497

Desserts and Baking

Healthy eating does not necessarily mean that all treats and desserts have to be cut out of the diet. As long as a sensible balance is maintained, there is no need to feel guilty about finishing a meal with something sweet. Desserts and cakes do not have to be high in fat and Calories to be full of flavour and as this chapter demonstrates, there are plenty of healthy, but delicious ideas for desserts and tea breaks.

Apricot and Banana Compôte

125 g/4 oz dried apricots
2 bananas
2 teaspoons lemon juice
25 g/1 oz raisins
150 ml/¼ pint low-fat natural yogurt
honey, to taste (optional)
grated nutmeg

wash the apricots, put them into a bowl and cover with cold water. Leave to soak overnight.

slice the bananas and toss in the lemon juice. Place the apricots in a bowl with a little of the soaking liquid. Add the bananas and raisins, then divide the fruit between 4 serving dishes.

sweeten the yogurt with honey, if liked, spoon over the fruit and sprinkle with grated nutmeg. Chill before serving.

Serves 4
Preparation time: *15 minutes, plus soaking and chilling*

FACT FILE • Keep bananas at room temperature until they are sufficiently ripe to use. You can save time by using no-soak apricots in this recipe.

carbohydrate 33 g • *protein 4 g* • *kJ 616* • *Kcal 145*

Lychee and Apricot Compôte

425 g/14 oz canned lychees
175 g/6 oz dried or Hunza apricots
2 large oranges
2 tablespoons pine nuts, toasted

drain the lychees and make the liquid up to 300 ml/¹/₂ pint with water. Put the apricots into a saucepan, pour over the liquid, cover and bring to the boil. Turn off the heat and leave to soak for 1 hour. Bring to the boil again, covered, simmer gently for 10 minutes and leave to cool. Turn into a glass bowl with the lychees.

pare off thin strips of orange rind with a potato peeler and cut them into needle-fine shreds. Blanch in boiling water for 1 minute, then drain and dry on kitchen paper.

peel the oranges with a serrated knife and cut into segments, removing all the membrane. Add to the bowl and mix together gently.

sprinkle the fruit with pine nuts and orange rind and serve chilled.

Serves 6
Preparation time: *20 minutes, plus soaking and chilling*
Cooking time: *20 minutes*

FACT FILE • Hunza are delicious baby apricots from the Hunza valley in northern India. They are much sweeter than ordinary dried apricots, so you may need to add a little lemon juice.

carbohydrate 31 g • protein 3 g • kJ 668 • Kcal 158

Tropical Fruit Salad

2 kiwi fruit, peeled and sliced
1 starfruit, sliced
2 mangoes, peeled and cubed
1 small papaya, peeled and cubed
6 lychees, peeled
1 banana, sliced
shredded rind of 1 lime, to garnish

Dressing
25 g/1 oz sugar
100 ml/3½ fl oz water
2 tablespoons lime juice
pulp and seeds of 2 passion fruit

first make the dressing. Put the sugar and water in a saucepan and heat until the sugar has dissolved. Add the lime juice and simmer for 5 minutes. Remove from the heat and set aside to cool. When the dressing is cool, stir in the passion fruit pulp and seeds.

gently mix all the prepared fruit in a large bowl. Pour the dressing over the fruit and chill for 15 minutes. Serve garnished with lime shreds.

Serves 4–6
Preparation time: *15 minutes, plus chilling*
Cooking time: *7 minutes*

FACT FILE • Kiwi fruit are quite high in Vitamin C, about the same as that of oranges, weight for weight. Fruits have varying contents of Vitamin C, with blackcurrants and guavas amongst the highest and plums and grapes amongst the lowest.

carbohydrate 35 g • protein 2 g • kJ 614 • Kcal 144

Yogurt
with Figs and Passion Fruit

2 passion fruit
250 ml/8 fl oz Greek yogurt
1 tablespoon clear honey
4 fresh figs
mint sprigs, to decorate

cut the passion fruit in half, scoop out the seeds and mix with the yogurt and honey.

cut each fig into 4 segments, peeling the fruit first if preferred. Serve the figs with the yogurt mixture and decorated with mint sprigs.

Serves 4
Preparation time: *10 minutes*

FACT FILE • Figs contain Vitamins A, B and C. They also have digestive properties.

carbohydrate 12 g • protein 5 g • kJ 494 • Kcal 118

Peach Granita

375 g/12 oz ripe peaches
150 ml/¼ pint dry white wine
150 ml/¼ pint orange juice
2 egg whites
redcurrants, to decorate (optional)

remove the skin from the peaches. Halve the fruit, removing the stones and chop the flesh roughly.

put the peach flesh into a saucepan with the white wine and orange juice. Simmer gently for 5 minutes, then blend the peaches and the liquid in a blender or food processor until smooth. Leave to cool. Put the mixture into a shallow container. Freeze until the granita is slushy around the edges, then tip into a bowl and break up the ice crystals.

whisk the egg whites until stiff but not dry. Fold lightly but thoroughly into the partly frozen granita. Return to the container and freeze for 2–3 hours until firm. Serve decorated with redcurrants, if liked.

Serves 4
Preparation time: *15 minutes, plus freezing*
Cooking time: *6 minutes*

FACT FILE • This type of iced dessert is very refreshing on a hot summer day or perfect for a barbecue. The peaches and fresh orange juice provide enough natural sweetness to make it unnecessary to add any artificial sweeteners.

carbohydrate 10 g • protein 3 g • kJ 309 • Kcal 73

Burgundy Peaches

1 orange
3 tablespoons clear honey
125 ml/4 fl oz water
1/2 cinnamon stick
1 clove
grated rind of 1/2 lemon
300 ml/1/2 pint red Burgundy wine
4 large peaches, peeled, halved and stoned, or canned peaches in natural juice
1 tablespoon arrowroot or cornflour
mint sprigs, to decorate

pare the rind from the orange and reserve, and squeeze out the juice.

place the honey, water, cinnamon stick, clove and orange juice in a large saucepan. Add the lemon rind and a thin strip of orange rind. Cover and bring to the boil over a high heat. Add the wine and peaches. Bring back to the boil, reduce the heat and simmer for 20 minutes.

when the peaches are tender, lift them out of the cooking liquid with a slotted spoon and allow to cool slightly. Slice each peach half and fan out the segments.

blend the arrowroot with a little water until smooth. Stir it into the cooking liquid and bring to the boil, stirring continuously until thickened. Strain the sauce into a jug. Pour a little of the sauce on to 4 individual dessert plates. Divide the peaches between each plate and decorate with pieces of the cinnamon stick and mint sprigs.

serve hot or well chilled.

Serves 4
Preparation time: *20 minutes*
Cooking time: *25 minutes*

FACT FILE • Honey has been used as a natural sweetener for many centuries. Honey has a higher fructose content than cane or beet sugar, but in nutritional terms it is little different from any other sugar. The traces of pollen present in honey may cause an allergic reaction in a small number of very allergic children.

carbohydrate 31 g • *protein 2 g* • *kJ 749* • *Kcal 176*

Baked Cranberry Pears

4 large, ripe dessert pears, peeled but with the stalks in place

250 g/8 oz cranberries, thawed if frozen

1 tablespoon chopped hazelnuts

3 tablespoons clear honey

150 ml/¼ pint dry white wine

few drops of red food colouring

mint sprigs, to decorate

working from the base and using a small teaspoon, scoop out the pear cores. Chop 2 tablespoons of the cranberries and mix with the nuts and 1 tablespoon of the honey. Press the mixture into the pear cavities.

put the remaining cranberries, honey, wine and a few drops of red food colouring in a flameproof dish and bring to the boil over a moderate heat. Simmer for 5 minutes. Stand the pears upright in the dish and spoon the wine over them.

cover the dish lightly with foil and cook in a preheated oven at 200°C/400°F/Gas Mark 6 for 30 minutes, basting the pears with the wine once or twice. Serve hot or cold, decorated with mint sprigs.

Serves 4
Preparation time: *20 minutes*
Cooking time: *40 minutes*
Oven temperature: *200°C/400°F/Gas Mark 6*

FACT FILE • Cranberries have a low sugar content and they are rich in Vitamin C. Cranberry juice contains an active ingredient (hippuric acid) which many people find helps reduce the pain and discomfort of cystitis.

carbohydrate 31 g • protein 2 g • kJ 950 • Kcal 226

Summer Pudding

500 g/1 lb mixed blackberries and blackcurrants

3 tablespoons clear honey

125 g/4 oz raspberries

125 g/4 oz strawberries

8 slices wholewheat bread, crusts removed

low-fat yogurt or yogurt snow, to serve

(see Cook's File, below)

Decoration

redcurrants

mint sprigs

place the blackberries, blackcurrants and honey in a heavy-based saucepan and cook gently for 10–15 minutes until tender, stirring occasionally. Add the raspberries and strawberries and leave to cool. Strain the fruit, reserving the juice.

cut 3 circles of bread to fit the base, middle and top of a 900 ml/1½ pint pudding basin. Shape the remaining bread to fit around the sides of the basin. Soak all the bread in the reserved fruit juice.

line the bottom of the basin with the smallest circle of bread, then arrange the shaped bread around the sides. Pour in half of the fruit and place the middle-sized circle of bread on top. Cover with the remaining fruit, then top with the largest bread circle. Fold over any bread protruding from the basin.

cover with a saucer small enough to fit inside the basin and put a 500 g/1 lb weight on top. Leave in the refrigerator overnight. Turn on to a serving plate and pour over any remaining fruit juice. Serve with low-fat yogurt or yogurt snow, if liked, and decorated with redcurrants and mint sprigs.

Serves 8
Preparation time: *30 minutes, plus soaking and chilling*
Cooking time: *15 minutes*

COOK'S FILE • To make yogurt snow, whisk 2 egg whites until stiff, then whisk in 3 tablespoons clear honey and continue whisking until very thick. Carefully fold in 300 g/10 oz natural yogurt and serve immediately, instead of cream.

carbohydrate 25 g • protein 4 g • kJ 490 • Kcal 115

Wholemeal Pear Tart

1 tablespoon clear honey, warmed, to glaze
redcurrants, to decorate

Pastry
100 g/3¹/₂ oz plain flour, sifted
100 g/3¹/₂ oz wholemeal plain flour
100 g/3¹/₂ oz sunflower margarine
2–2¹/₂ tablespoons cold water

Filling
2 tablespoons raspberry jam (optional)
2 teaspoons custard powder
¹/₂–1 tablespoon caster sugar
150 ml/¹/₄ pint skimmed milk
425 g/14 oz canned pear halves in natural juice, drained

to make the pastry, place the flours in a mixing bowl. Rub in the margarine until the mixture resembles fine breadcrumbs. Add water, mix to make a firm dough and knead until smooth. Roll out two-thirds of the pastry to a circle large enough to line an 18 cm/7 inch greased flan ring.

trim the edges from the ring. Place in the refrigerator for 10–15 minutes to chill. Prick the base of the pastry case with a fork and bake blind in a preheated oven at 200°C/400°F/Gas Mark 6 for 10 minutes. Leave to cool, then spread the jam, if using, over the pastry base.

to make the custard, blend the powder and sugar with 1 tablespoon of the milk in a small bowl. Bring the rest of the milk to the boil in a small saucepan and pour it over the custard, stirring until thickened and smooth. Pour the custard into the flan and allow to set slightly. Arrange the pear halves around the edge of the pastry, rounded sides up.

roll out the remaining pastry to fit the flan ring. Dampen the edge of the pastry base. Place the pastry top on the flan and press gently to seal the edges. Trim and flute the edges. Bake in the oven for 30–40 minutes.

remove the flan ring and brush the tart with honey. Serve decorated with redcurrants.

FACT FILE • Pears are a source of Vitamins B and C and they also contain potassium.

Serves 6
Preparation time: *30 minutes, plus chilling*
Cooking time: *40–50 minutes*
Oven temperature: *200°C/400°F/Gas Mark 6*

carbohydrate 43 g • protein 5 g • kJ 1303 • Kcal 310

Fruit and Nut Crumble

175 g/6 oz dried apricots
125 g/4 oz dried pitted prunes
125 g/4 oz dried figs
50 g/2 oz dried apples
600 ml/1 pint apple juice
100 g/3½ oz wholewheat flour
50 g/2 oz margarine
50 g/2 oz muscovado or soft brown sugar, sifted
50 g/2 oz hazelnuts, chopped
low-fat yogurt, to serve (optional)
rosemary sprigs, to garnish

place the dried fruits in a bowl with the apple juice and leave overnight to soak. Transfer to a saucepan and simmer for 10–15 minutes, until softened. Turn into an ovenproof dish.

sift the flour into a bowl and rub in the margarine until the mixture resembles breadcrumbs. Stir in the sugar, reserving a little to serve, and the hazelnuts, then sprinkle the crumble over the fruit.

bake in a preheated oven at 200°C/400°F/Gas Mark 6 for 25–30 minutes. Serve with low-fat yogurt, if liked, sprinkled with the reserved sugar and garnished with rosemary.

Serves 6
Preparation time: *15 minutes, plus soaking*
Cooking time: *35–50 minutes*
Oven temperature: *200°C/400°F/Gas Mark 6*

FACT FILE • Dried fruit such as apricots and prunes add to the iron content of the diet. Absorption of iron is aided by Vitamin C, but inhibited by a number of other factors, including tea-drinking.

carbohydrate 41 g • protein 2 g • kJ 950 • Kcal 226

Hazelnut Meringues

with Raspberries

2 egg whites
125 g/4 oz icing sugar, sifted
50 g/2 oz hazelnuts, finely chopped
strawberry or mint leaves, to decorate

To serve
500 g/1 lb raspberries
125 ml/4 fl oz whipping cream, whipped
icing sugar, to dust (optional)

whisk the egg whites until stiff and dry. Add the icing sugar a tablespoon at a time and continue to whisk until very thick.

carefully fold in the hazelnuts. Pipe the meringue mixture on to a non-stick baking sheet in swirls.

bake in a preheated oven at 180°C/350°F/Gas Mark 4 for 15–20 minutes. Leave to cool slightly, then transfer to a wire rack to cool.

serve the meringues with the raspberries and whipping cream, decorate with herb sprigs and dust with icing sugar, if liked.

Serves 6
Preparation time: *15 minutes*
Cooking time: *15–20 minutes*
Oven temperature: *180°C/350°F/Gas Mark 4*

FACT FILE • There is very little nutritional difference between white and brown sugars. Brown sugar contains small traces of some minerals, but its main function in the diet, as with all sugars, is to add a pleasant sweetness to food.

carbohydrate 26 g • protein 3 g • kJ 680 • Kcal 160

Nutty Orange Flapjacks

125 g/4 oz sunflower margarine
50 g/2 oz demerara sugar
2 tablespoons clear honey
175 g/6 oz rolled oats
25 g/1 oz chopped nuts
finely grated rind of 1 orange
orange rind, to garnish

heat the margarine, sugar and honey in a medium saucepan over a low heat, stirring with a wooden spoon until the ingredients have melted together. Remove the pan from the heat.

stir in the oats, nuts and orange rind. Mix well and spoon into a greased 18 cm/7 inch square shallow tin, pressing down lightly.

bake in a preheated oven at 190°C/375°F/Gas Mark 5 for 25 minutes. Leave to cool, easing the cake away from the sides of the tin with a sharp knife while still warm.

when cool, cut into squares and serve garnished with orange rind.

Makes 9 squares
Preparation time: *10 minutes, plus cooling*
Cooking time: *30 minutes*
Oven temperature: *190°C/375°F/Gas Mark 5*

FACT FILE • Honey contains about 80% glucose and fructose sugar and traces of calcium, potassium, magnesium and phosphorus, but no vitamins.

carbohydrate 17 g • *protein 2 g* • *kJ 662* • *Kcal 158*

Applenut Spice Squares

125 g/4 oz plain flour
1 teaspoon bicarbonate of soda
$^{1}/_{2}$ teaspoon ground cinnamon
pinch of ground cloves
50 g/2 oz sunflower margarine
125 g/4 oz golden granulated sugar
1 egg, beaten
50 g/2 oz walnuts, coarsely chopped
75 g/3 oz sultanas
150 ml/$^{1}/_{4}$ pint apple purée (made from
500 g/1 lb cooking apples)
icing sugar, to dust (optional)

sieve the flour, bicarbonate of soda, cinnamon and cloves into a mixing bowl and mix together. Work in the margarine lightly. Mix in the sugar and beaten egg. Add the walnuts, sultanas and apple purée and blend well. Pour the mixture into a greased and lined 18 cm/7 inch square tin.

bake in the centre of a preheated oven at 180°C/350°F/Gas Mark 4 for 45–50 minutes, or until firm to the touch. Cut into squares. Serve cold, dusted with icing sugar, if liked.

Makes 9 squares
Preparation time: *15 minutes*
Cooking time: *45–50 minutes*
Oven temperature: *180°C/350°F/Gas Mark 4*

FACT FILE • Walnuts have a high fat and protein content. They are also a good source of Vitamins B and D.

carbohydrate 34 g • protein 4 g • kJ 1079 • Kcal 258

Orange and Sultana Fruit Loaf

200 ml/7 fl oz skimmed milk

I teaspoon bicarbonate of soda

50 g/2 oz sunflower margarine

200 g/7 oz plain flour, sifted

25 g/I oz bran

¹/₂ teaspoon ground cinnamon

125 g/4 oz soft brown sugar

250 g/8 oz sultanas

50 g/2 oz walnuts, chopped

rind of I orange

2 tablespoons orange juice

Topping

25 g/I oz walnuts

grated rind of I orange

2 tablespoons marmalade, melted

blend the milk with the bicarbonate of soda in a small bowl. Combine the remaining loaf ingredients in a mixing bowl. Add the milk and beat together with a wooden spoon for 5 minutes.

spoon the mixture into a greased and lined 500 g/1 lb loaf tin and smooth the surface. Bake in a preheated oven at 160°C/325°F/Gas Mark 3 for 2 hours or until a clean skewer inserted into the loaf comes out dry. Turn out on to a wire rack.

arrange walnuts over the top of the loaf, scatter with grated orange rind and brush with the melted marmalade. Allow to cool completely before slicing.

Makes 1 x 500 g/1 lb loaf
Preparation time: *15 minutes, plus cooling*
Cooking time: *2 hours*
Oven temperature: *160°C/325°F/Gas Mark 3*

FACT FILE • Wheat bran is an excellent source of insoluble fibre, which aids the rapid passage of food residue through the gut. It is slow transit of food residue through the gut which causes constipation. Pure wheat bran is best used in foods and not taken on its own.

carbohydrate 59 g • protein 6 g • kJ 1495 • Kcal 355

Cinnamon and Date Scones

250 g/8 oz plain wholewheat flour
4 teaspoons baking powder
2 teaspoons ground cinnamon
pinch of salt
50 g/2 oz butter or margarine
50 g/2 oz muscovado sugar
75 g/3 oz dried dates, chopped
175 ml/6 fl oz milk and water mixed
extra flour, for rolling out

sift the flour, baking powder, cinnamon and salt into a bowl, adding any bran left in the sieve. Rub in the fat, then add the sugar, dates and milk. Mix to a dough, then turn out on to a floured board and knead gently for a minute or two; the consistency will be sticky and soft.

place the dough on a lightly floured board and roll or pat out to a thickness of 2 cm/¾ inch. Cut out the scones using a 5 cm/2 inch round cutter. Put the scones on a baking sheet and bake in a preheated oven, 220°C/425°F/Gas Mark 7, for 10–15 minutes, until risen and firm. Cool on a wire rack. Serve warm.

Makes 12
Preparation time: *20 minutes*
Cooking time: *15 minutes*
Oven temperature: *220°C/425°F/Gas Mark 7*

FACT FILE • Dates have a high sugar content and are eaten mainly for their flavour. Fresh dates contain some Vitamin C, but this is lost in drying and storing. Both fresh and dried dates contain Vitamins of the B complex, although they are not major sources in the diet.

carbohydrate 22 g • protein 3 g • kJ 537 • Kcal 127

Date and Walnut Bread

125 g/4 oz breakfast bran
75 g/3 oz molasses sugar
125 g/4 oz dates, chopped
50 g/2 oz walnuts, chopped
300 ml/½ pint milk
125 g/4 oz wholemeal flour
2 teaspoons baking powder

put the breakfast bran, sugar, dates, walnuts, reserving some dates and walnuts to decorate, and milk in a mixing bowl. Stir well and leave for 1 hour. Add the flour, sift in the baking powder and mix together thoroughly.

turn the mixture into a lined and greased 500 g/1 lb loaf tin and sprinkle over the reserved dates and walnuts and bake in a preheated oven at 180°C/350°F/Gas Mark 4 for 55 minutes–1 hour, or until a skewer inserted into the centre of the loaf comes out clean. Turn out the loaf on to a wire rack to cool.

Makes 1 x 500 g/1 lb loaf
Preparation time: *15 minutes, plus standing*
Cooking time: *55 minutes–1 hour*
Oven temperature: *180°C/350°F/Gas Mark 4*

FACT FILE • Many proprietary breakfast cereals are fortified with a number of vitamins and minerals, making them a very useful addition to the diet. Cereals fortified with Vitamin D are particularly useful for people who may not be able to get the vitamin from sunlight.

carbohydrate 40 g • protein 7 g • kJ 953 • Kcal 225

Wholemeal Bread

1.5 kg/3 lb wholemeal flour
50 g/2 oz fine oatmeal
1 tablespoon salt
25 g/1 oz fresh yeast
900 ml–1.2 litres/1½–2 pints warm water
2 tablespoons malt extract
2 tablespoons oil
2 tablespoons rolled oats

mix the flour, oatmeal and salt in a bowl. Mix the yeast with a little of the water and leave until frothy. Add to the flour with the remaining water, malt extract and oil and mix to a smooth dough.

turn the dough on to a floured surface and knead for 8–10 minutes until smooth and elastic. Place in a clean bowl, cover with a damp cloth and leave to rise in a warm place for about 2 hours, until doubled in size.

turn on to a floured surface, knead for a few minutes, then divide into 4 pieces. Shape and place in 4 greased 500 g/1 lb loaf tins. Brush with water and sprinkle with the oats.

cover and leave to rise in a warm place for about 30 minutes, until the dough just reaches the top of the tins. Bake in a preheated hot oven at 220°C/425°F/Gas Mark 7 for 15 minutes.

lower the temperature to 190°C/375°F/Gas Mark 5 and bake for a further 20–25 minutes until the bread sounds hollow when tapped underneath. Turn on to a wire rack to cool.

Makes 4 x 500 g/1 lb loaves
Preparation time: *20 minutes, plus rising*
Cooking time: *35–40 minutes*
Oven temperature: *220°C/425°F/Gas Mark 7,* then *190°C/375°F/Gas Mark 5*

FACT FILE • Dried yeast can be substituted for fresh yeast in bread recipes, but as it is concentrated only half the amount should be used.

carbohydrate 21 g • *protein 4 g* • *kJ 455* • *Kcal 107*

Walnut Soda Bread

500 g/1 lb wholewheat flour
2 teaspoons baking powder
1 teaspoon salt
1 tablespoon light muscovado sugar
75 g/3 oz chopped walnuts
300 ml/½ pint natural yogurt
water, to mix
2 tablespoons milk
2 tablespoons cracked wheat

sift the flour, baking powder and salt into a mixing bowl and stir in the sugar and walnuts. Stir in the yogurt and sufficient water to make a firm yet pliable dough.

knead the dough lightly in the bowl until it is smooth and free from cracks. Shape the dough into a round about 18 cm/7 inches in diameter and place it on a greased baking sheet. Brush the top with milk and sprinkle with the cracked wheat.

bake the loaf in a preheated oven at 180°C/350°F/Gas Mark 4 for 40 minutes, or until it is well risen, firm and sounds hollow when tapped underneath. Cool on a wire rack.

Makes 1 x 18 cm/7 inch round loaf
Preparation time: *15 minutes*
Cooking time: *40 minutes*
Oven temperature: *180°C/350°F/Gas Mark 4*

FACT FILE • Cracked wheat or bulgar wheat includes wheatgerm and is therefore rich in carbohydrate and protein. It is produced by cooking the wheat, allowing it to dry and then cracking it.

carbohydrate 18 g • protein 4 g • kJ 480 • Kcal 114

Index

Acknowledgments

Special photography by Simon Smith

All other photos:
Octopus Publishing Group Ltd. / William Lingwood, Jean Cazals,
Chris Crofton, Philip Dowell, Laurie Evans, Sue Jorgensen, Graham
Kirk, Sandra Lane, Fred Mancini, Hilary Moore, Vernon Morgan,
Roger Philips, Roger Stowell, Clive Streeter, Philip Webb, Paul
Williams

Home economists
Lucy Knox and Sarah Lowman